Creating a
College Culture
for
Latino Students

Creating a
College Culture
for
Latino Students

Successful Programs, Practices, and Strategies

Concha Delgado Gaitan

CORWIN
A SAGE Company

CORWIN
A SAGE Company

FOR INFORMATION:

Corwin
A SAGE Company
2455 Teller Road
Thousand Oaks, California 91320
(800) 233-9936
www.corwin.com

SAGE Publications Ltd.
1 Oliver's Yard
55 City Road
London, EC1Y 1SP
United Kingdom

SAGE Publications India Pvt. Ltd.
B 1/I 1 Mohan Cooperative Industrial Area
Mathura Road, New Delhi
India 110 044

SAGE Publications Asia-Pacific Pte. Ltd.
3 Church Street
#10-04 Samsung Hub
Singapore 049483

Printed in the United States of America.

A catalog record of this book is available from the Library of Congress.

ISBN 9781452257709

Acquisitions Editor: Dan Alpert
Associate Editor: Megan Bedell
Editorial Assistant: Heidi Arndt
Production Editor: Amy Schroller
Copy Editor: Kimberly Hill
Typesetter: Hurix Systems Pvt. Ltd.
Proofreader: Joyce Li
Indexer: Jeanne R. Busemeyer
Cover Designer: Anupama Krishnan
Permissions Editor: Karen Ehrmann

This book is printed on acid-free paper.

MIX
Paper from
responsible sources
FSC® C014174

FSC
www.fsc.org

12 13 14 15 16 10 9 8 7 6 5 4 3 2 1

Contents

Acknowledgments

I am appreciative to Corwin's editors Dan Alpert for his guidance and encouragement and Heidi Arndt for her assistance. On the home front, I am grateful to my husband, Dudley Thompson, for his support and to my friend Debra Ratner for thinking aloud with me.

Publisher's Acknowledgments

Corwin gratefully acknowledges the contributions of the following reviewers:

Margaret Adams
Director of Language, Literacy and Title I
Malden Public Schools
Malden, MA

David Bautista
Superintendent
Woodburn School District
Woodburn, OR

Margarita Calderón
Professor Emerita
Johns Hopkins University
Washington, DC

Nelia Correa-Patrick
Teacher
Walsh Middle School
Framingham, MA

About the Author

Concha Delgado Gaitan, PhD, is an award-winning ethnographic researcher and professor of sociocultural studies in education. She received the George and Louise Spindler Award for her contributions to the field of Anthropology and Education from the Council of Anthropology and Education of the American Anthropological Association. Her early career as a teacher and school principal informs her later work as a practicing anthropologist in communities and professor at the University of California, Davis. Concha has also worked in the field of public health education in Latino communities, combining that interest with her dedication to issues of social justice and education. She is a national and international speaker as well as a consultant on the numerous topics that inspire her work.

Among her many scholarly publications are her books where she presents her work as an ethnographer working with disenfranchised families and communities toward their empowerment and extending practical lessons to educators: (1) *The Power of Community,* (2) *Protean Literacy,* (3) *Crossing Cultural Borders,* (4) *Literacy for Empowerment,* (5) *School and Society,* (6) *Involving Latino Families in the School,* (7) *Building Culturally Responsive Classrooms,* and this most current one (8) *Creating a College Culture for Latino Students.* In a different book, *Prickly Cactus,* she turns the lenses inward to look at the role of family and community in her life during a time of major health crisis. Concha works and lives in the San Francisco Bay area with her husband, Dudley Thompson. For more information, please go to www.conchadelgadogaitan.com or contact Concha at itsmecdg@yahoo.com.

To Drs. Carmen and Reynaldo Contreras for their tireless commitment and work, who along with other progressive educators, dedicated families, and communities, have led countless students to achieve their highest goals and dreams.

Introduction

1

ON MY WAY TO COLLEGE

I begin with my personal story to illustrate how some Latinos get socialized to attend college.

Before my junior year in high school, I do not recall hearing the word *college* in a way that seemed meaningful in planning my future. I disliked school since elementary school. I loved learning, but I did not like school. However, good grades were my incentive. Not only did my parents expect it, but also I think I liked the competition. My parents instilled a strong work ethic that transferred to the way I approached learning in school. Discipline, responsibility, and working conscientiously were the underlying principles. Although they spoke limited English, my parents trusted my sisters and me to keep track of our academic progress because we, not they, knew how schools worked. In spite of that, Mom showed up at every school meeting and insisted that we always work to the best of our ability.

During middle and high school, I was a good student but I always had to fight my way out of remedial classes. The Iowa Standardized Test scores determined students' placement in academic classes. I always scored at the lowest of my peer group. Following the reporting of the test scores, my high school counselor called me into her office and shared with me my results. I always placed 99th percentile on mechanical ability. Nice, if I wanted to work in a garage, but my low academic scores in language placed me in remedial classes.

Every first week of fall classes, I found myself nodding off in the remedial language arts class where the teacher stood in front of the class and dictated a list of spelling words such as "truck" and "baseball." I looked around the class and my classmates were falling asleep with their heads on their desks. Although my mother did not have the opportunity to attend high school, she always taught us to advocate for ourselves. So I inevitably ended up in the office of the high school counselor, Mrs. Nichols. I complained about the boring class and reminded her that I had always received good grades in the advanced English and literature classes. She looked up my file and said, "Oh, we do need to get you into another class." She always found a spot for me in the advanced classes. After my mother's expectation of me to advocate for myself, the credit goes to Mrs. Nichols. If she had paid attention only to my standardized test results, I would never have been able to demonstrate that I could master advanced coursework.

I loved the challenge in my physics, literature, and trigonometry classes. When trigonometry felt like a bigger challenge than I could handle, my father tutored me. He had not even finished first grade in Mexico because he was stepping over dead bodies on his way to school during the revolution.

I was a junior in high school when my older sister was preparing to graduate from high school and planning to attend a local college, but we didn't talk much about her actual college experience. At school, college was the only conversation among my friends. Teachers prepared us for the SAT tests, and counselors advised students on how to apply for college. Lunchtime talks with my friends sounded overwhelming and confusing as they shared their excitement and fears about applying to the colleges that their parents wanted them to attend. I just listened and felt relieved that I wasn't going to have to go through all that stress. Although I was an excellent student, loved learning and studying, and like my friends, was in the Scholastic Society and the top of our class, college was not in my plans. We were all in the Scholastic Society, top of our class, but college eluded me. I did not have plans to attend college.

I intended to graduate and continue working at Bullock's Department Store, where the manager in our department had invited me to be her assistant. I also planned to marry my high school boyfriend at some point. Mrs. Nichols changed all that when she called me into her office. She said that I was in the top ten of our graduating class and that Whittier College, a local private college, was offering scholarships to the top ten students in our graduating class, allowing us to take interesting college classes during our senior year. It was an opportunity for us to take classes that might interest us and become acquainted with college life.

I was never one to shy away from a challenge, so I jumped on board. In my senior year, I had enough units to graduate and could take advantage of the offer that Whittier College made to us. I took a sociology class and loved the readings and class discussions.

The Whittier College experience stirred my curiosity about attending college after graduating. Occidental College seemed like a good place to go because it was within commute distance, so I applied. Again, Mrs. Nichols called me into her office with news. "The University of the Pacific (UOP) in Stockton is offering a four-year scholarship to a bilingual student interested in majoring in InterAmerican Studies at their Covell College, an experimental international program. You're a very good student and if you apply, I think you have a good chance of getting the award."

My head exploded with questions beginning with, where is Stockton? "Near Sacramento," said Mrs. Nichols. That was my opportunity to leave smoggy Los Angeles. Sure, I loved my family, but the idea that someone might pay me to explore worlds away from Los Angeles thrilled me. Oh, what I could learn! The scholarship was for tuition and room and board. I would still have to work part-time for my personal needs. . . . Not a problem. I was not a stranger to work.

My mother agreed that I should apply, but we didn't tell my father for fear that he would squelch my dream. He was not in favor of his daughters moving out of home unless it was for marriage. By now, I had put that plan to rest.

At the time, finances were very tough for my family, so I didn't feel comfortable asking them for the money for the application. I saved a little bit from my part-time job, but it wasn't enough for the fee. When I shared that with my English teacher, she loaned me $50.00 for the application. I paid her back the following week with my check from my part-time job at Bullocks.

Within a few weeks, I received an acceptance letter from Occidental College. They accepted me but only offered a very small scholarship. I didn't respond to their offer until I heard from University of the Pacific (UOP). That letter arrived two weeks later. They accepted me and offered me a full four-year academic scholarship with one condition—that I would main-tain above-average academic standing. Tears filled our house that night, mine with excitement and my parents with dread. They knew I couldn't turn down such an opportunity, but noth-ing prepared them for letting me go. They kept asking me why I couldn't attend a local college like my older sister. No explana-tion satisfied them. My mother accompanied me to the meet-ing when the UOP recruiters visited our area. The meeting was important because we both got to understand a bit more about what college life offered and what it meant to live in a dorm and the work opportunities available.

Dad had to work, so he couldn't drive me up to college in the fall. My mother, her friend and I packed up my boxes and I took the Greyhound bus up eight hours north to Stockton. The real shock was when I arrived in Stockton, where the 108 degree heat and the less-than-attractive Greyhound station overwhelmed me. Suddenly, I longed for Los Angeles. But UOP's lovely brick-and-ivy buildings quickly restored my excitement. After that ini-tial visit to the Greyhound station, I would revisit it many times when I made trips home to visit my family. My tight student bud-get sometimes meant that I had to donate blood for $5.00 each time I had to buy a Greyhound ticket. It was worth it because I had to heal my fractured relationship with my father, who disliked the idea of me being so far from home. But years later, when he attended my graduations from UOP then Stanford, he couldn't be prouder that his daughter had college degrees.

When did you first hear the word *college*? Did you hear it from your parents? From a high school counselor? When did you first decide that you were going to college? Who helped you to make your decision? How did you know what college you wanted to attend? If your parents did not have college experience, who coached you on the road to college? How did you choose your major and your career goals? All these questions lead us to ask, whose responsibility is it to socialize, orient, and prepare students to successfully pursue college?

The subject of getting underrepresented Latinos to college is of great concern for me. Working in Latino communities has taught me that we need to get the next generation of Latinos to college and into profes-sions that can raise the well-being not only of their own families but also of the community at large. My professional roles as a teacher, principal, educational and community ethnographic researcher and professor at the University of California have given me the privilege to hear countless stories that together comprise a portrait of the educational situation that Latinos face getting to college. Along the way, I have become convinced that understanding the college experience begins before students enter kindergarten. Therefore, the school's role in socializing Latino students to college must begin the minute they enter school. This does not mean that students cannot learn about the college process later in middle and high school; it means that Latinos whose parents do not have the educational background have some catching up to do with parents who socialize their children for college from birth. By reaching parents, they reach other children in their families and help prepare students so that the responsibility does not all rest on educators. The education cycle, including students, educators, and parents, needs to be cohesive. Thus, explicit messages about college must begin as early as possible. Some schools as well as local and national programs have found ways to intervene and redirect this trend with Latino students.

The world economy is dependent on the fields of technology and science. That is also the direction of the U.S. economy and in which Latinos must be fully prepared to participate. Schools need to increase the number of students entering college. Currently, four out of ten mainstream students enter college. Many students who have not had opportunities to attend college are Latinos from below-poverty-level households, where parents are not college graduates. California is one of several states where Latinos are the largest growing group. Latino students in California now constitute the majority in public schools. Although they are the fastest growing group in the United States (Gándara, 2010; U.S. Census, 2010), they are the least likely to attain a college degree. The grim reality is that without a college degree, secure employment in the workforce becomes less attainable since entry requirements have escalated.

Achieving college readiness has become a national imperative. Reinforcing that point, Charles Reed, Chancellor of the California State University system, stated that 44 percent of jobs in the current job market require a baccalaureate degree. Given that reality, by the sixth grade, students should be prepared for college (Reed, 2010). In their recent, best-selling book, journalist Thomas Friedman and professor Michael Mandelbaum (2011) argue that a strong U.S. economy requires investment in the education of all students, including those who need more supports to succeed, because they are the future workforce. Students must be prepared to attend college both for themselves and to strengthen the economic system.

The talents of many young students go unrecognized when we fail to create supportive paths to get them there. To help get Latino students enter and graduate from college, we need to institutionalize a path for them to follow. We need to raise consciousness among students, educators, and parents through creating systemic approaches in the school curriculum and clear avenues for students to follow from elementary through high school.

An explicit goal of the Common Core State Standards is to ensure that every student achieves college and career readiness. In a knowledge-based economy, the most desirable careers demand the higher order thinking skills that are emphasized in the Common Core. Whether a student chooses to attend college or not, the underlying assumption of the Common Core is that she should be fully prepared to enter college upon graduating high school (Burris & Garrity, 2012; National Governors Association Center for Best Practices, Council of Chief State School Officers, 2010). Socializing students toward college encompasses certain key pillars; among them, cultivating an academic, social, and emotional environment where educators' high expectations support accelerated academic practices such as tutoring and mentoring services that partner with families and communities. These activities constitute a college culture. Incorporating college culture in the K–12 standards prepares students to enter college and pursue twenty-first-century careers.

Various lifelong factors contribute to the obstacles that Latino students face in considering college. *Lifelong* is an appropriate term to describe the process required for students to know what is expected of them on the path to college. That process spans from the time they are toddlers to the time they receive their college admission letter. Students' whose parents have attended college have an advantage where preparing their children for college is concerned. By the time some of these students begin preschool, they have been told that they will be attending college. Some have already selected a college. Even if some children may not understand the full significance, we hear them boast excitedly about their decision.

Unfortunately, with few exceptions, the educational system is not fully organized to address college preparedness until high school. However, by high school, Latino students' post–high school future may have already been decided for them. They have either been tracked toward college or a nonacademic direction. Students who are not in college-bound classes are unlikely to apply for college. This is often the case for all students who may be academically weak before high school because if they do not qualify for advanced classes they are academically unprepared for college. Many of these students become emotionally defeated having remained in remedial classes for much of their schooling. Thus, dropping out of school becomes easier. While these conditions apply to various ethnic groups from low-socioeconomic communities, the focus of the book is on underserved Latino students because they are the largest growing group in the United States.

Educators and families need to work together to promote the highest student achievement. Parental values play a major role in shaping their children's academic success, choices for college, and pursuit of a career. Going to college is unquestioned in many families. But among Latinos from underrepresented communities, students may feel unprepared for college. They may not have the academic preparation to socialize their children by instructing them to make appropriate academic decisions. Students may come from families whose parents have not attended college. Those parents may want their children to attend so that they can improve their options for employment. Students whose parents are unfamiliar with the educational system and ways to prepare them for the long road ahead need to seek extra support from educators and community members. Even if some students are academically advanced, they will not attend college without the necessary support.

In spite of this gap between the knowledge about college and the resources, there are Latino parents who support their children emotionally and encourage them to stay in school and succeed academically because they believe that during hard times in one's life, no one can take your education from you. Their strong message to their children conveys a belief that when you have an education you have more choices in life. Parents' hopes emerge from an expectation and faith that their children will break the cycle of poverty in their family.

The heart of this book builds on the premise that it is imperative that Latinos attend college and build human capital—the workforce. Effective academic and social support practices intertwine with increased expectations, successfully leading underrepresented Latino students to college and nurturing human capital. Connectedness of cultural, emotional, informational, and instrumental networks undergirds students' readiness and aptitude. In this way, students avail themselves of all the possible academic and social opportunities provided to them to seek resources outside of their immediate settings. Building on theses notions, children need to begin seeing themselves college bound as early as kindergarten.

ON WRITING THIS BOOK

One of the most inspiring parts of writing this book has been hearing the personal stories and experiences of students, educators, and family members involved at various levels of preparing students to college. Personal story plays an important role in putting a good face on the situation at hand. After all, stories are about people's real-life experiences, how we communicate with each other, how we perceive our status in our communities, and how we make meaning of our educational experience that leads us to our future career. Some parents work two or three jobs to help their child to be the first to realize the dream of going to college. Educators, too, maintain hopes for these students that others might dismiss. The power that all their stories hold helps us uncover common ground and understand that we can collaborate to create a strong road for students to follow from their early years until they reach the college doors.

Wherever possible throughout the text, I include personal narratives of students, parents, and/or educators' perspectives and experiences. In all the stories that I collected, I use pseudonyms because that was my agreement with all the people interviewed. Many stories throughout the book were collected during various research projects that began with a larger educational focus. Others came from independent interviews that my research assistants and I conducted in several states where I had access to students, educators, and parents, including California, Texas, Illinois, Iowa, Colorado, Utah, Massachusetts, and Washington, D.C. I tried to obtain interviews representative of small and large schools as well as from urban, suburban, and rural areas. One exception to using pseudonyms is first-person narratives from the Internet where individuals listed their real names. In those cases, I cited the source.

As important as college is as a destination, the process is equally critical. Furthermore, it is very complex and should be one that is discernible for students whose parents do not have a history of college in their family. In my story, we see that Mrs. Nichols is a supportive counselor. Yet the fact that I, as an excellent student in advanced classes, made it to the eleventh grade without much information about college and the complicated application process implies that the school expected students to understand the college application process independently. How did my friends know all about college as they discussed where they would apply? Their parents were professionals or they were knowledgeable about college and were able to coach. Other important players in my story are my Latino classmates in those remedial classes that I was able to leave and they stayed. No one advocated for them. They probably felt the same way I did in that classroom—bored and uninspired to learn. But that's what happens when the educational system disempowers students. By the time they reach high school, they have given up. My classmates and I shared an ethnicity and a socioeconomic status—living in the same neighborhood. However, the difference was that I had family and friends around me that would not let me feel beaten down. I had people who encouraged and challenged me. There is no substitute for a personal cheering squad that believes in the student's potential, regardless. That I loved learning helped. And that is teachable.

Family support, socioeconomic conditions, social networks, and supportive school personnel are key components in a student's path to college. Although I was one of the first to attend college in my family that does not mean that my parents did not support the idea of college. From our early school years, Mom involved herself in everything she could, including Parent–Teacher Conferences, Back-to-School Night and countless other parent events at school to stay on top of our performance. Dad, with his knowledge of math, was an incredible tutor for me. Although his fear during the Mexican Revolution robbed him of opportunities to attend school, he had innate intelligence. Their support held us to high expectations to get a career. In our family, education had a purpose beyond employment that included proper conduct in and out of the family, good work ethic, learning as much as you can, and being a valued citizen in one's workplace and community. Certainly, that was my mother's constant reminder to my sisters and me.

AFTER THIS INTRODUCTION

Eight more chapters follow this introduction. They do not provide recipes for how schools should do "schooling for Latinos." Instead I have three major goals: (1) for educators to reflect on the importance of preparing Latino students for college; (2) to offer examples and lessons from certain communities that show how educators deal with this need; and (3) to describe successful partnerships that schools, nonprofit organizations, and university collaborations have fashioned to facilitate the path to college. Below is a preview of the chapters. Throughout the book, I will call the reader's attention to some key questions that educators can ask themselves about their own setting. I also include specific details that emphasize the crux of the story from various settings. Here's a preview of the chapters to come.

Chapter 2: Influences in Getting Latinos to College

A disproportionately large percentage of Latinos live in conditions of poverty and Latino boys and girls attend low-performing, underresourced schools. These circumstances present obstacles that preclude them from succeeding in public schools and consequently from pursuing postsecondary education. I'll present the most salient of these conditions.

Chapter 3: Promising Educational Practices

Specific educational practices promote the necessary academic and social conditions for getting Latino students to college. They include (1) high expectations; (2) the goal of college attendance; (3) promoting rigorous course taking and academic excellence; (4) college tours, visits, or fairs to help students from elementary and secondary levels better plan for college; (5) parental involvement as a goal; and (6) early outreach beginning as early as fourth grade. These practices invite personal stories about students' experiences in creating maximum learning opportunities.

Chapter 4: Talking College in Elementary School

In the absence of systematic elementary-level curriculum for orienting students toward college, educators, including teachers, principals, and counselors, describe their efforts to shape self-esteem in Latino students along with academic and career planning.

Chapter 5: College Readiness in Middle and Secondary School

Transitioning from middle school to high school is a critical part of ensuring students' success on their path to college. Students have opportunities to participate in college-bound programs. I describe specific pillars necessary for strengthening students' academic achievement, such as school programs, including the Breakthrough Collaborative that sometimes partners with nonprofit organizations. I highlight lessons that schools and communities can integrate into their educational programs.

Chapter 6: Features and Activities of Successful Programs

Key nonprofit programs have a strong reputation for succeeding in preparing students for college. Among these programs are Upward Bound, Advancement Via Individual Determination (AVID), East Bay Consortium (EBC), and the Breakthrough Collaborative. Public schools can glean important lessons from these projects to incorporate into their school curriculum such as mentor programs, parent involvement, and tutorials.

Chapter 7: Collaborations and Partnerships

Public schools establish effective partnerships with nonprofit organizations to help Latino students get to college. The four programs discussed here, Hidalgo Independent Schools, Puente, and GEAR UP, represent different models of operation. Although schools and nonprofit programs differ widely in the way they organize their collaboration, educators can glean important guidance from the different partnership models.

Chapter 8: College Planning With Parents

Parents of Latino students often find schools intimidating, making it difficult to learn how to best support their children to get to college. On the other hand, teachers and other school personnel feel that they would like to communicate more closely with parents but are often unsuccessful. Here I present what parents tell me they would like from the schools. In turn, I share what successful teachers do to engage parents to join with them in helping students prepare for college.

Chapter 9: Students Navigating the College Culture

Personal and emotional information about college issues may not always make it into traditional college guides. Sometimes students without a family tradition of college experience may not even know the questions to ask. This chapter provides a resource for school personnel to address Latino students' needs. I include sample questions around fears of failure, family approval, and of some wisdom that students say they need as they prepare for college. School personnel can provide information to Latino students through various means, including informational workshops, written guides, study groups, and college counseling.

Chapter 10: Sites for Educators, Students, and Families

Websites and other contact sites are included in this chapter.

References

This section lists the references cited in the text.

NOTE TO THE READER

My decision to describe the educational trajectory of Latinos is intentional; it is a way to explore more in-depth, historically and culturally, how one ethnic group of students navigates their way to college. The reader will notice, however, that much of the discussion throughout this book is also applicable to other groups who face obstacles in getting to college. They too would benefit from effective, supportive programs that challenge them to reach for the rungs on the ladder to attain their goal—college.

Influences in Getting Latinos to College

2

A college education has never been more important. . . . Eighty-nine percent of the new jobs created in this economy will require post-high school levels of literacy and mathematics. . . . The typical worker with a college degree makes 73 percent more (than workers without).

—U.S. Department of Education cited in First
Generation College Bound, Inc., 2012

GEOGRAPHIC, CULTURAL, AND SOCIOECONOMIC CONDITIONS

Influences for Patricia

Patricia was a hardworking student through her elementary, junior high, and high school years. She stayed up late almost every night completing homework and studying for tests. Patricia always earned good grades but does not remember ever visiting with a school counselor about her career interests or the classes she should take to enter college. Patricia also did not talk to her parents about her high school classes, future plans, and career interests because she felt that they probably could not counsel her on these matters. She reported that the classes that she took were due to her interest in being an accountant—an easy job to find. Consequently, in high school she was placed in a noncollege track course of study. Patricia motivated herself to make all her career decisions on her own. Counselors never reached out to her in high school.

When Patricia was a junior, she had a friend, Linda. After school, she went to Linda's house and loved it when her friend's mom came home.

Linda's mom was a teacher and she liked watching her come in the house with a bag full of work to prepare for her class.

I watched my friend's mother carry in her bag of schoolwork to grade and set up bulletin boards. I got excited to see that she was doing something that was important—teaching young children. That seemed like something that I might want to do. Still, I didn't change my classes or anything in high school. I just kept studying hard for the classes that I was taking to work as an accountant after high school. When I left high school, I knew I would go to the community college because I wanted to be as prepared as I could get in the area of accounting. So, I looked into one of the local community colleges and filled out an application.

Patricia took all the liberal arts classes, and at the end of the two years, she decided to continue studying in college. She transferred to a four-year state college, and after graduating with a B.A. in Spanish literature, she pursued a credential and a master's in education to teach elementary school.

This interview with Patricia took place after she graduated with her doctorate from the University of Illinois as part of a group of doctoral graduates I contacted because I wanted to know about Latino students' routes to and through college. Given their high school experience, had they received mentoring? Who supported them in the choices and application process? Patricia does not blame her high school counselors for tracking her into a noncollege course and not guiding her in her choice of classes. Nevertheless, a problem exists when Latino students are allowed to cruise through high school without any intervention on the part of the counselor, especially if they can coach students about college. No doubt Patricia was self-motivated and searched out the classes she needed in high school and college toward her goals. Although she does not describe her high school experience as a noncollege tracked program, hers was indeed a tracked situation.

Some would say that she tracked herself into a noncollege course because she did not take advanced science and math classes in junior high school or high school. Thus, she could not qualify to apply for a four-year college. When Patricia realized that she might like being a teacher as Linda's mother was, could a counselor have intervened and assisted her to chart a path to getting to a four-year college? Why didn't Patricia contact her high school counselor? Did she not see the connection between what the counselor could offer and her career interest? The issue is that Patricia should be applauded for her strong self-motivation to choose a career such as accounting because she was at least thinking practically—that she could become economically independent from her parents. And changing to a teaching career shows even more initiative on her part as well as confidence to pursue her heart's desire. The role of educators, however, is critical in assisting students to shape their coursework to coordinate with their career choices. This is not to minimize the value of accounts' work no two-year community colleges. Yet Patricia's story corroborates too many Latino students' stories about the way they have to navigate inadequate guidance in high school at a time when students need the full encouragement of all adults in their lives to consider a career and get through the college application process.

Where Latinos Live, Work, and Study

The evening news frequently reports on the rapidly growing Latino population in the United States. The 2010 census counted 50.5 million Latinos in the United States, comprising 16.3 percent of the total U.S. population. The overall nation's Latino population, which was 35.3 million in 2000, grew 43 percent over the decade. Latinos also accounted for most of the nation's growth—56 percent—from 2000 to 2010. Young people under age 18 make up over 20 percent of that increase.

In this age of global commerce and networking, where employment depends largely on workers with advanced technological knowledge and skills, the stakes are higher than ever for entering and completing college. Not only are employment opportunities much more abundant for college graduates, but the lifetime financial returns for them are at least twice what high school graduates earn (Cabrera & La Nasa, 2000). However, access to college for many Latino students from low-socioeconomic families remains a distant dream, especially for Latinos whose families live in low-socioeconomic communities.

Geographically, most Latinos live in nine states that have large, long-standing communities—Arizona, California, Colorado, Florida, Illinois, New Mexico, New Jersey, New York, and Texas—but the population in other states has been growing. In 2010, 76 percent of Latinos lived in these nine states, compared with 81 percent in 2000 and 86 percent in 1990. There are more Latinos living in Los Angeles County (4.7 million) than in any state except Texas.

Although a large number of U.S. counties have experienced growth in numbers of Latinos, most of the increases have occurred in the southern and western states, according to a 2008 Pew Hispanic Center report

(Fry, 2008). The Pew report found that of those in the highest Latino growth areas of the United States, approximately 30 percent are children. Sixty percent of families have an immigrant as head of household. Approximately 35 percent speak limited English. Fifty-seven percent of Latinos report having completed high school compared to 78 percent of non-Latinos (Koebler, 2011; Lopez, 2009).

This diversity is reflected in the college plans of the Latino high school students. Some Latino youth resembled other college-prep students from upper-middle-class families nationwide: For them, college attendance is a foregone conclusion. Others may want to attend college but are hindered by a myriad of obstacles. They come from families with no tradition of college attendance. Many of these students are unprepared academically, and by their own report had little likelihood of attending college. This group poses a major challenge for the school system. If they do attend college, they are the first in their family to do so.

By 2050, Latinos will comprise 29 percent of the entire U.S. population (Pew Hispanic Organization, 2008). Proportionately, this is bound to increase the preschool–12 Latino student enrollment (Chapa & De La Rosa, 2004). For the most part, Latino youth ages 16–25 feel optimistic about their futures and place a high value on education, hard work, and career success (The Pew Hispanic Organization, 2011). Yet they are much more likely than other American youths to drop out of school and to become teenage parents. Findings of this age group matter here because these are students in and out of America's public schools, moving into adulthood in this society. It's also important to note here that there is a disconnect between the way that many Latino students feel about their lives and the reality of preparedness and performance in the real world.

Fry (2006) reports that about 28 percent of Latino students in public schools live at or below the poverty level. Their families typically earn less than $22,000 annual income. This represents a disproportionately large percentage of Latinos compared with non-Latinos (including Asians and Whites) living in such conditions. They attend low-performing, underresourced schools, presenting obstacles that prevent them from succeeding in public schools and consequently from pursuing postsecondary education.

In some Latino communities, students drop out of school at the rate of over 40 percent. National figures show that only 10 percent of Latinos who go on to college actually graduate from a four-year institution. Researchers (Allen, Bonous-Hammarth, & Suh, 2003; Immerwahr & Foleno, 2000) document numerous reasons for this dismal portrait. Poor schools and programs for poor students who speak a language other than

English, unprepared teachers, low expectations on the part of educators, and alienation of parents from schools rank among the top explanations for the students' educational failures. Each of these educational break-downs is discussed in the following sections.

Poor kids attend poor schools—Schools confront a Herculean mission educating students from low-income communities. Even controlling for everything else, socioeconomic status remains the highest predictor of achievement (Verdugo & Glenn, 2006). Whereas all students deserve the best possible educational opportunity, large groups of culturally diverse students from marginalized low-socioeconomic communities remain underserved by the existing educational system. Within this group is a large Latino immigrant population with a complex history of discrimination and educational neglect, although many schools in poor communities have exceptionally strong teachers and administrators that work long hours overtime to help students perform on par to peers in affluent schools.

Although poverty alone does not cause academic failure, schools that are situated in low-socioeconomic communities influence student performance. Noguera and Williams (2010) note some general qualities about schools and poor communities. In such cases, the researchers specify three ways: less money is spent on the per-pupil spending which bears on the quality of facilities, the lack of available updated materials, and the inability of schools to retain high-performing teachers and administrators; students with special needs have social, emotional, and psychological needs that go unmet because of lacking funds; and schools serving large numbers of poor children need larger and more specialized resources.

Although nationally student access to well-resourced, high-performing schools is available to 17 percent of Latino students, these students compete with 32 percent White students who attend the similar high-performing schools. Conversely, poor students often attend fiscally impoverished schools. Findings by the Schott Foundation for Education (Schott Foundation for Public Education, 2009) provide a national overview showing that 35 percent of Latino students as opposed to 15 percent of White students attend poorly resourced, low-performing schools. Poorly financed schools create a chain effect of dysfunction. This is evidenced as experienced teachers avoid teaching in those schools, attracting mostly inexperienced teachers. Furthermore, inadequate buildings prevent teachers from expanding new and creative programs. Dated and scarce books and materials frustrate teachers, students, and parents. The problem is exacerbated when schools alienate parents from participating in their children's education, reinforcing ignorance about the school and diminishing student support.

Students have a lot *to* say about their high school experience. Haycock's (2001) research asked low-income, underrepresented children, What about the things that adults are always talking about, neighborhood violence, single-parent homes, and so on? Students responded, *"Sure those things matter, but what hurts us more is that you teach us less"* (p.3). These are powerful insights from those who matter. Many other students exit school before schools can quantify them, so it is impossible to ascertain how they feel about school.

How to improve these school failures spurs heated debates. Professor and advocate Pedro Noguera, and the Broader, Bolder Approach in Education Project (BBA) believe that better schools are more likely to result from dealing with the poverty that afflicts many students (Noguera, 2008). Educational reform executive, reporter, and charter school advocate Joe Williams of the Education Equality Project (EEP) believes that we're more likely to get better schools by focusing on what can be controlled within the walls of the school. Success is also possible within the boundaries of the district, such as measuring school progress, paying teachers for excellence, giving students choices of where they want to attend, and concentrating on the broader issues of poverty. Ultimately, it is possible for poor children to achieve at high levels when educators create accelerated conditions for learning. And how educators perceive Latino students plays an important role in creating optimal conditions.

Whose expectations matter?—The National Center for Education Statistics reports that Latino students are more likely to leave school before completing a high school program than White students. However, Latinos are the fastest growing group in the nation's elementary and secondary schools (Fry & Gonzalez, 2008). As we are all very aware, the problem begins at the K–12 levels. Urban cities face a bigger problem with respect to underachievement resulting from low expectations of educators. The issue of low expectations and the self-fulfilling prophecy effect is well documented. According to Darder (2012), teacher expectations related to lower class and bicultural students can result in teachers being more likely to hold negative expectations for these students rather than for middle-class White children. These expectations are extended to other members of the educational setting such as guidance counselors. As quoted by Darder, the following students' remarks on this issue speak to what some Latino students confront.

Javier: "My guidance counselor, for example, felt very strongly that I should not attend any four-year institution for that matter. A second incident comes to mind in which I asked a teacher if I could go to the library to complete a scholarship application and he indicated that it was a waste of my time."

Noemí: "On my own I decided to apply for college late in my senior year or like a shot in the dark because I didn't have any options after high school. I did the work myself and hoped for the best."

Lynnette: "The major challenge I confronted was not feeling completely prepared for college, compared to students who were in the Classical Magnet Program."

Fine (1991) stated, "Students who begin with the greatest economic disadvantages receive the least enriching education and end up with fewer, less valuable, and historically deflating diplomas" (p. 26). In that way, educators' low expectations undermine students' full potential.

Unprepared Teachers

The issue of "expectations" calls to question the broader picture of qualified teachers teaching underrepresented students. *Unprepared teachers* describes best what happens in the classrooms that undermines academic performance. Teachers too often endure the most blame when students fail academically as though they were independent agents, when in fact, teachers are part of an educational system that prepares and credentials them. Novice teachers typically arrive at schools without having made decisions about the curriculum they are held accountable for teaching. The needs of Latino students in underserved communities have needs that surpass training. Students' language needs require teachers to know not just how to teach English to students who speak Spanish, but they also need to create an inclusive interactive classroom climate that organizes English speakers and English learners (EL) to communicate with each other.

Not all Latino students are EL students. However, even when students are not EL and speak English as their dominant language, most need a great deal of language support to make them competitive with their non-Latino English-speaking counterparts. Hand in hand with knowing how to address the language issues of EL students is the teacher's ability to understand the students' home culture. Too often, when students fail to perform well academically, they fault the students' family and cultural life.

Whatever appears different from the mainstream culture that governs the classroom gets interpreted as the family's failure to provide for their children the necessary mainstream orientation to succeed academically in the classroom. Actually, it is the classroom culture that needs to change. A culturally responsive classroom encompasses parental engagement inclusive policies and well-prepared teachers. Qualified teachers for English learners play a central role in teaching Latino students. Today, nearly 50 percent of classrooms have at least one English learner in their classroom. The National Center for Educational Statistics found that most teachers of EL felt unprepared to meet the students' needs (National Center for Educational Statistics, 2012). The responsibility for preparing teachers to teach EL students rests not only on public school district educators but also on university programs.

Families Seeking Opportunities

As is true in all cultures, there is no single Latino family type. Latinos are as diverse as any other ethnic group. Mexican, Mexican American, Chicano, Central Americans, Latin Americans, Puerto Ricans, Dominicans, and Cubans comprise identities within the Latino population in the United States.

For Latinos, education has been more than an avenue of socialization; it has been a stage of power struggles between the immigrant group and the English-speaking mainstream group with competing political interests. Latino students who face severe obstacles on their way to college may come from immigrant working families. The news media regularly report incidents involving Latino workers. If this is the main source of information that people have about Latinos in the United States, they might imagine that the majority are undocumented persons sneaking across the border to steal jobs from U.S. citizens. However, this picture blurs the fact that most Latinos are fully documented, hardworking law-abiding citizens contributing to society.

Like the cultural heterogeneity among Latinos, social-class standing also varies. Latino workers in the United States are not just housekeepers—the "help" and the "leaf blowers." They are judges, architects, professors, university presidents, journalists, doctors, business owners, governors, athletes, and scientists. While many highly visible professionals of Latino heritage work and reside across the country, many remain relegated to working-class status as agricultural workers, factory workers, and paraprofessional service providers. Recent immigrants are most likely found in these entry-level jobs. They immigrate with high hopes of expanding educational opportunities for their children, which can lead to economic betterment.

Family Alienation and Aspirations

The National Center for Public Policy and Higher Education Public Agenda conducted a survey where Latino, African American, and White parents were asked if they believed that college was necessary for future success. Of the three groups, the Latino ranked highest (65 percent) in their response to the question on whether a college education is necessary for success even if the adults had not been to college (Immerwahr, 2003). Although Latino parents were more likely to emphasize the importance of getting a college education, Latino students are significantly less likely to complete either a two-year or a four-year degree (Fry, 2000).

Latino families desire their children to maneuver successfully within the social system involving extended family members in settings where they live, study, and work. Education is the vehicle to accomplish this very feat. The family as a social unit holds a valued place as a resource for coping with life's stress. Its preservation is critical to the continuity of social, political, religious, and cultural order. As in all ethnic groups, the family is the primary social unit among Latinos. Configurations of family life include two-parent families, extended families with grandparents, uncles or cousins, and single-parent families. The extended family also plays a very strong role. Close family ties depict how family members relate to each other whether family lives in the same household or resides outside in another country. Traditional values and practices are transmitted in Latino families that maintain strong family ties. Schools can tap these values. Parental authority and respect are highly valued and considered a form of love. Children are expected to take instruction from parents without questioning. While total acceptance of authority may not be the best classroom practice, educators' awareness of these values provides insights to creating effective learning settings.

Contrary to many educators' perceptions, Latinos value education. They want their children to succeed in school in order to obtain better employment than they have. This globalization era affects Latino immigrants such that youth are required to develop marketable skills, sensibilities, and strategies of thinking that exceed what the current U.S. educational system delivers. These generations of historical, social, and cultural distance between the schools and the Latino community must be bridged. This is possible only through systematic outreach to Latino community leaders, to Latino religious and social organizations, and to Latino families to make them an integral part of the decision-making voice of the school.

Typically, parents of higher socioeconomic background participate more regularly in the schools even if the schools do not encourage parent involvement. Attending school in the United States gives them familiarity with the school system. They know how to access resources for their children. On the contrary, immigrant parents often face alienation from schools. Some educators believe that parents who have not been educated in the Untited States, or if they speak Spanish only, are deficient in their ability to support their children's education. However, successful schools collaborate with immigrant communities to support students' schooling. When schools and families collaborate to enrich the educational program, they advance students' opportunities to grow, adjust, and benefit academically, moving them along the college path.

Although many immigrant Latino parents do not understand the educational programs, they count on their children receiving a good education. The responsibility is on the educational system to retain Latino students in school and support them to graduate from high school and college. Part of that responsibility means bridging strong and meaningful relationships with Latino families and communities. High aspirations are a critical rung in the ladder toward college since often Latino students are inclined to believe that they are prepared for college (Boden, 2011). In a Pew study (Swail, Cabrera, & Lee, 2004), non-Latino eighth-grade students aspire to receive a bachelor's degree at an 80-percent rate. Aspirations appear dimmer for Latinos compared to any of their counterparts. Only 55 percent of eighth-grade Latino students aspire to complete a bachelor's degree. In fact, by eighth grade, 27 percent of Latino students have left school. The disparity lies in that Latino parents lack the information or resources to advocate for resources toward their children's educational goals. Thus, the school's role matters greatly in preparing Latino students toward college; educators and families need more support to achieve their goals. That preparation must begin the minute students start school.

Many argue that schools continuously fail many students across all groups. If that's the case, immigrants and other ethnically diverse students face more dismal school conditions. Parents with familiarity of educational system can support their children in their schooling more so than those who are unfamiliar or alienated from the U.S. schooling experience. That is, students' academic success depends on the entire family's ability to participate meaningfully in their children's schooling.

MAJOR HURDLES

Even when Latino students are academically strong, they often face challenges that, if not addressed, they may not get to the door of their favorite college. Although obstacles may be labeled differently, the underlying message of all these categories is that students cannot do it alone.

Adult Guidance

High school students comment that they do not receive much guidance from educators or from parents during their high school years when they need to make serious decisions about their college choice and need guidance in filling out applications.

For students unfamiliar with the college application process, they may become easily confused as to what it means to choose a college. For example, some often believe that they must choose a career before applying for college. Others have interests but are vague about what a full career entails; that often discourages them from even applying for college in the first place.

Work First

How do you convince students whose families depend on them financially to forgo their plans for full-time work and attend college? One of the deterrents that Latino students face on their way to college is the obligation to work full-time after high school. Latino students whose families live in low-socioeconomic conditions face a great deal of pressure to live at home, work locally, and help support the family. If students are unable to contribute financially, they are often expected to assist by helping with younger siblings and the care of family members with health problems. Unfortunately, deferring college plans often means that students find work more comfortable than returning to the discipline of studying academics. This makes it too easy for students to remain in low-paying jobs and dismiss the idea of attending college.

REFLECTIONS

The urgency of the educational system to address college preparation for Latino students is underscored by Harry Pachon, Professor of Public Policy at the University of Southern California. He states, "The future is now in terms of challenges presented to school districts across the nation by this influx of Latino youth." He elaborates, "A large percentage of these students are U.S. citizens by birth." Of significance is that the first graders that Pachon refers to will largely remain in the public schools and continue into colleges and universities, requiring a culturally responsive educational system to succeed academically. Additionally, these students have families that also need strong social and educational structures to support their children's education (Cardona, 2009).

Rodolfo de la Garza, Professor at Columbia University and Vice President of Research at the TRPI, observes,

> This is a profound demographic change, which provides a challenge for American education, just as European immigrants created a new foundation for New York through their ambition to excel and succeed. Latinos, if provided [educational] support will be in a position to strengthen our cities and our nation.

Garza asserts that the educational system needs to develop comprehensive educational programs for Latino students (Cardona, 2009). Furthermore, he proposes an education that advances the group's civil rights.

No single practice promises Latino immigrant students and other refugee groups a rewarding educational experience. Comprehensive school programs that actualize language and cultural equity, well-prepared teachers, effective school leaders, and progressive family and school partnerships maximize opportunities for Latinos to achieve academically and actualize personal and social change in their own lives and that of their communities.

3

Promising Educational Practices

HIGH EXPECTATIONS FOR SAL

Salvador grew up with immigrant parents in a small agricultural community. He, like many other Spanish-speaking students, was relegated to the lowest reading group, not because he couldn't read but because he was limited in his English-speaking ability. Sal read Spanish at home and according to his parents, he was quite competent in his first language. The disadvantage for him in his school was that there wasn't a bilingual program where he could progress in his reading skills while learning English. The school policy dictates that Spanish-speaking students should not speak Spanish in school; rather, they should be taught in English only.

Sal recalls that by the fifth grade, he and his peers were quite bored in school. They did not feel challenged. Their boredom led to discipline problems in school among him and his peers. This became the norm. Sal only looked forward to going to school so he could get in trouble with his friends because they tried to outwit the teachers. On one occasion, when he was sent to the principal's office, the principal told him that all he wanted from him was that he stop causing problems for his teacher, and he couldn't wait for him to leave that school. Sal remembers feeling very shamed. He settled down a bit, trying to pay attention in class. He says that he even raised his hand sometimes because he knew the answer, but the teacher never called on him. Sal tells how alone he felt in school. He couldn't find a way to get engaged in learning. "I didn't like school and school didn't like me either," Sal recalls.

Finally, it was time for sixth grade. His teacher was Mr. Torres, the only Latino teacher in their small neighborhood school. This was Sal's opportunity to start a clean slate and try to fit in school. Mr. Torres called on Sal when he raised his hand and even when he didn't. He placed him in a higher reading group in English for which Sal felt quite proud. He recalls that his parents were also proud, telling him that they knew he could do better.

One day Sal and his friends were acting out in class and Mr. Torres said, "Sal, this isn't like you. I expect more from you." At that point, Sal says he understood that a teacher actually cared about him and his behavior. His conduct and academic performance improved dramatically because he now felt that someone cared and held him accountable for his behavior. Mr. Torres expected him to "do better."

It wasn't too late for Sal. He advanced in his academic work such that he began planning the career he'd like to have after graduating. No surprise, he wanted to be a teacher like Mr. Torres, who became his mentor into high school. Sal graduated with honors and attended the community college close to home, then he transferred to the state university and became a celebrated teacher in the community. He committed himself to developing programs for limited English-speaking students. Later he became a school principal. Eventually, he earned a doctorate.

Sal's story illustrates the power of high expectations for students whose experience with low expectations undermines their academic performance. Up to the point that Sal met Mr. Torres, he usually met up with educators who thought less of his abilities and potential. Although his parents wanted him to do well, they were not equipped with the experience or knowledge to sustain Sal's enthusiasm for schooling. Teachers leave an enduring impression on students, motivating and challenging them to rethink their feelings of self and perform to a higher promise.

CRAFTING A COLLEGE CULTURE
TO SOCIALIZE STUDENTS FOR COLLEGE

Students need socialization in order to be prepared for college admission. To accomplish this involves creating a college cultural environment encompassing academic, social, and emotional programs and support. Certain educational mainstays provide the backbone for informing and encouraging students along their path to college. The important pillars include high expectations, college/university visits, career days, tutoring, mentors, parent engagement, community outreach, school support groups, and the college application process (Immerwahr, 2003; Jager–Hyman, 2008; Perna, 2002; The Pathways to College Network, 2004).

Building High Expectations

What we expect from students is too often exactly what we get. And nowhere is it more true than in schools where educators' perceptions and expectations matter because they influence how students believe in themselves and how they are treated in the learning setting (Tauber, 1997). High expectations on the part of educators comprise a critical facet of college socialization and preparedness. Educators often attribute successes and failures to factors such as ability, effort, task difficulty, and luck. Teachers may project high expectations for the future if they believe that a student's success is due to his or her high ability and will attribute a high achiever's failure to bad luck. When a student's failure is attributed to low ability, a teacher begins to expect less in the future. Subsequent "lucky" successes of such students are unlikely to be considered as evidence that the low ability label should be changed. The question of expectation plays out as early as kindergarten when students begin with less academic preparation than their middle-class counterparts or as Molera (as cited in Immerwahr, 2003) identifies them, "college-prep" students. Latinos typically comprise the "noncollege-bound" students. They enter school with fewer financial resources and minimal meaningful parental support. This inequity gap widens over the years. As college-prep students receive necessary direction toward college from parents and educators, noncollege-bound Latino students find themselves in the opposite situation. Economic circumstances may force families to relocate frequently, forcing students to attend numerous schools, resulting in underachievement because of loss of motivation and increased truancy. These conditions minimize students' opportunities for academic enhancement especially when educators do not believe that they would ever qualify to attend college, continuing to perpetuate the gap between high and low expectation.

An example of how expectations play out in daily classroom practices occurs in teacher/student verbal exchanges. Particular classroom practices evidence how teachers convey their expectation toward Latino students from underachieving groups. When asking students a question, teachers tend to wait longer for non-Latino students to respond than Latino students. The classroom culture often requires teachers to move the discussion along and bypass students who delay in responding. Latino students have been observed as slower in responding, especially in science, not because they don't know the answer but because of the different linguistic patterns. This accounts for the fact that some students respond faster to the teacher's questions. Teachers, in turn, allow non-Latino students more time to respond to questions. Teachers need to observe the patterns of student/teacher interactions in their classrooms and recognize that Latino students may know the answers to question but require a little more time to respond. Sal's story at the beginning of this chapter illustrates how teachers generally expect less of students that are perceived to be underachieving (Losey, 1995; McKown & Weinstein, 2008; Tenenbaum & Ruck, 2007).

Typically Latino students do not receive systematic or sustained support for going to college from elementary through high school. The quality of occasional or sporadic information lacks the depth and breadth of knowledge, information, motivation, and inspiration that an ongoing, continuous process needs to provide. Just as students need consistent orientation, parents, teachers, and counselors also need ongoing support and training in working with Latinos. Educators need to consider Latino students' college potential even if they do not fit the preconceived image of a typical profile of a college-bound student. Parents of these Latino "potential college students" need coaching and education, enabling them to guide and direct their children from a knowledgeable position (Garcia, as cited in Immerwahr, 2003). Ultimately, students need enduring support from the time they enter kindergarten to the time they graduate from high school. A socialization path can take many routes but some key pillars have shown to be particularly significant.

School Career Days and College/University Visits

Pretending "what we want to be when we grow up" has been a fun childhood game, and schools play a critical role in helping students create a realistic plan to make their wish a reality. It's important to inspire young Latino students to picture themselves in professions such as nurse, architect, pharmacist, physical therapist, physician, engineer, and of course, teacher or librarian. This is not intended to undermine the jobs of Latino families in the community. Rather, it is about getting students to create a dream of a college-bound career that they can pursue in the future. All work is valuable if it contributes to the upkeep of the family. Students need to hear that message as they choose a career that will develop their full human potential.

Reaching for those rungs on the ladder begins in kindergarten. Teachers can start students thinking and looking forward to college by getting them to talk about what they envision themselves doing when they grow up. Latino students need to believe that they can attain a profession beyond the hourly wage jobs that may surround them in their community. Using picture books and stories, teachers acquaint young students with professions with which they may not be familiar. Books and stories introduce professions that teachers can follow up with by inviting professionals from the community to visit the classroom. Guests can conduct interactive "show and tell" presentations about their work, permitting teachers to expose students to real persons who hold jobs to which students may aspire. Another thing it accomplishes is motivating students who haven't thought about what people in their community do and how they became the professionals they are; they can begin thinking about the work that it takes to get to become an expert in their field.

Career days involve all students in classrooms, including non-Latino students. However, for Latino students from families in the lower socio-economics sector, these lessons are especially important. They provide a window of opportunity for students as they move up the grades. Once students can read and write, career days fit into the daily classroom literacy activities. Teachers can coordinate student discussions with research projects about certain professions. Students further inform peers through projects such as speeches, video explanations, posters, and even written stories about someone they interviewed.

In middle and high school, career fairs become more elaborate because students can assist educators to organize the fairs by deciding what professionals to invite. They're also able to help organize the information booths and choose the information they need. From the school, educators, including counselors, set up tables and booths with information on the application process. Getting students involved in the planning is particularly important for Latino students. They should be able to personally invite Latino professionals from the community and host them during the event. Also, if the invited professionals speak on the school auditorium stage, Latino students can introduce them. This gives them the opportunity to talk with the guests. These contacts can also lead to opportunities for students to shadow professionals in their respective workplaces.

Hand in hand with making early career choices is visiting colleges and universities, which is possible to begin as early as second grade. Some classroom teachers collaborate to take their combined grade-level students to local colleges and/or universities on field trips. Coordinating college visits with local universities is an advantage to higher education because they are expected to prepare the next generation for their dream careers. Getting underrepresented Latino students to walk onto a college campus breaks the fear and myth they harbor—that college is mysterious and unattainable. Teachers have reported that on a visit to the local college in the early grades, the Latino students are quite surprised to see students at the college engaging socially. They thought that college was all studying and no fun. Having students understand that building social networks in college is a critical aspect of university life is of great value. Some schools do Saturday visits. The advantage of Saturday college campus visits is that parents can accompany students. Schools obtain supplemental financial support through grants to visit colleges and universities.

Guest speakers, literacy lessons, class assignments, school career fairs, and college field trips can string together from kindergarten through high school to provide a systematic focus on the importance of choosing a career early in life for everyone, including students whose parents did not attend college.

Tutoring and Mentoring

Although tutoring and mentoring services may overlap in the roles they play in schools, here I distinguish mentoring from tutoring in that tutoring is a relationship that is usually based on academic skills. Tutoring is an opportune time to talk about college and encourage students to work toward that goal. Often, tutoring encompasses the academic; mentoring encompasses emotional and social skills orientation. However, other types exist; the most typical ones include peer tutoring and tutoring from expert adults. Good study habits are critical to academic success at any level, and peer tutoring provides that support. Jarsky, McDonough, and Nuñez (2009) observed older students mentor younger ones on organizational skills and other strategies. In their research, the middle school counselor also provides a type of mentoring by meeting regularly meet with students before school to ensure that their homework is completed and that their work is neat and organized. She or he reminds all of these students that they are college bound.

Latino students benefit from both forms of tutoring at all grade levels because they often need much more academic assistance than teachers or parents can supply. Elementary schools have been successful in contracting with local high schools to have older students tutor young students during the school day. How success is measured matters a great deal because, if underachieving students are to benefit from tutoring, the project should know what aspects are effective and which what aspects need to change. Successful cross-age tutoring programs are typically those that train the tutors and evaluate them (Powell, 1997). One factor in a successful tutoring program is matching peer tutors and learners. During tutoring, students should also receive counseling and problem solving to help learners constructively address their conflicts with teachers or peers. A way that schools can reduce the stigma of high-risk students receiving tutoring is to recruit and train them to serve a peer tutors. Schools that include high-risk students in their tutoring program report that those students experience confidence, prestige, pride-and positive feedback from others (Powell, 1997).

Some schools make agreements with volunteer adult experts in different subjects from the community to tutor after school. That schools can provide such tutoring for students is particularly important for Latino students that come from families with limited resources. These students compete with classmates whose families can afford tutoring services and have no problem picking up the phone and hiring a teacher to tutor their child after school or evenings. These parents have friends or family members who gladly step up to the task of tutoring the students and improving their academic outcomes.

Mentors hold a critical place in guiding Latino students academically throughout all of their schooling years. Generally, the positive effects of mentoring for Latino students include improved grades, test scores, improved motivation and attitude toward school, increased self-esteem and confidence, and familiarity with different settings (Reisner, Petry, & Armitage, 1989).

In her story, Ana tells how a mentor paved the way for her to become better informed about the classes to take and to think ahead. Ana's mother, Mrs. Avila, was a single parent raising four children; Ana was the youngest. Her older sibling had graduated from high school but had not attended college. Ana appreciates the fact that her after-school mentors since the fourth grade have helped her think about her skills and her ability.

I'm in the sixth grade now, and I love computers. I want to be a software engineer when I grow up. And the two college ladies that were my mentors that helped me at school told me that I have to work very hard so I can get to college and then become an engineer. That helped me because I didn't know that everything I study now is important for me to get into good courses in high school. For this dream, I guess that means that I have to work hard in school even now. In seventh grade, I will have to get used to the change because there are more teachers and using lockers. I also have to get to class on time and complete all of my assignments and my homework. Then in high school, I will study harder than ever so I can graduate and go to college.

My mother likes that I want to go to college, but she says that they can't help me pay for it, so I'll pay for my own classes. I'll take animation classes and I will work really hard on the computer, making good games and pictures. And when I get a software engineer job, I will have my own computer and desk; I will be the best designer in the state.

Step by step Ana is mapping out her career as a software engineer. By her accounts, the mentors clued her in about how the process of getting to college works. It is not that educators do not encourage students about college, but mentors have a one-on-one relationship that teachers may find impossible to build with students given the large classes. Not only students but teachers also benefit from mentors working with students. The mentor provides practical information that students may miss in their daily schooling and is necessary for them to keep working toward long-range goals. Ana recognizes the changes ahead with middle school, where classes will be more difficult. She seems able to rely on and listen to the coaching that mentors provide as well as the support and encouragement that her mother extends as she hears about Ana's plans to attend college.

Mentoring programs take different forms. Depending on the availability of professionals in the community, some mentoring efforts are organized by individual teachers while others involve the entire school. To assist students in tutoring and mentoring programs, elementary schools write grants. Mentors do not receive financial compensation, but schools hold special events such as informational events or career days with the students they mentor. Middle and high schools build partnerships with universities to develop mentoring programs with university students mentoring Latino students. This relationship further expands the opportunity for Latino students to visit colleges as part of their mentoring activities.

The Berkeley Scholars to Cal (BSC) program exemplifies the strength of mentors in preparing students for college. Since its inception in 2000, there have been four cohorts of students who are the first in their families to attend college. BSC enlists students in the fifth grade and mentors them on through high school. Teachers submit the names of promising fourth graders to BSC. Students are required to make a commitment to remain active for eight years. They receive comprehensive intervention, including ongoing case management, mentoring, Saturday, after-school and summer academic enhancement. An evaluation report (Belohlav & Brown, 2012) on the second cohort together in the fifth grade and now in the eleventh and twelfth grade, indicates that their academic outcomes have enhanced students' possibilities for entering college. Primary activities, including coaching, case management, summer academies, college tours, and mentoring, teach students to become independent scholars and self-advocates. Cal students act as mentors and role models for the young students, paving the way for them to apply to Berkeley or other top-tier higher education institutions.

According to evaluation reports, the BSC cohort improved academically in contrast to the comparison group. The BSC group spends more time on homework. They're better able to overcome academic difficulties and are more likely to identify college attendance as their top goal after high school. The first two behaviors are positively related to student GPAs and standardized test scores. Furthermore, the students' time spent in the program positively influences their behavior and attitudes among student participants. By comparison to the control group, BSC have a 3.3 GPA (vs. 2.27 for control group). Before going to college they perform at the 80th percentile on their SAT, which is above the 50th percentile and higher than their White counterparts nationally. After graduation, 100 percent of BSC graduates attend one of the University of California campuses, a California State University campus, or a private college.

As in every effective educational program, parents play a key role in BSC. Parents attend a monthly meeting with other parents. Since Alexa joined Berkeley Scholars in 2011, her father said that she has become more confident, and now sets targeted goals. Alexa's brother, Chris, a fifth grader, called his sister "a role model" (Edelstein, 2010). The BSC program changes student behavior and ultimately guides students academically and socially from fifth grade on to college.

FRAMING CULTURE THROUGH ACTION RESEARCH

Various models of effective college cultures are possible. Building on her research project, McDonough (2005) proposes a "college culture from elementary through high school" as a way to socialize underrepresented students toward college. Through McDonough's team work with feeder elementary schools in Los Angeles, McDonough (2009) discovered that students with college awareness as early as kindergarten are aware of and aspiring to college. Given the need for early college socialization, McDonough suggests a set of principles for a college culture that extends from K–12. Schools with a college culture focus their energy on building consciousness about college. They make time to talk about college preparedness in all staff development and parent meetings. Furthermore, resources are devoted to the broad goal of college preparation for all students, not only the top achievers. More specifically, where such a college culture exists, structural, motivational, and experiential college preparatory opportunities promote college socialization and preparedness.

A school college culture evolves from the conditions where key personnel are fundamentally committed, including school leadership that are compelled to organize a college culture; all school personnel convey a consistent message to students that supports their quest for a college preparatory K–12 experience; all counselors serve as college counselors, and counselors, teachers, and families collaborate to prepare students for college. These characteristics are derived from decades of research on college access and educational attainment and are designed to allow schools to determine the extent to which they are currently fostering a college culture and the steps they might take in the future to strengthen that culture, which some states have taken steps to implement (Casvanagh, 2005).

Educators need to create a climate conducive to learning. In this environment, communication is often nonverbal. Regardless, affective and cognitive feedback must be provided to learners. "Input" is increased as teachers teach more to students of whom they expect more. "Output" is also increased as teachers encourage greater responsiveness from students for whom they hold high expectations.

In addition to the above practices that orient students toward college academically, socially, and emotionally, McDonough (2009) suggests other principles for college socialization that broadens the breadth of the college preparedness process. She labels her list "Principles of Building a College Culture." McDonough conducted a case study of 27 Los Angeles Unified School District middle and high schools in 2001. McDonough and her team collaborated with the LA Unified School District and The Achievement Council to identify how schools create a college culture that assists students and their families in discerning their path to college. Among McDonough's college culture list are

- parent engagement
- college talk
- comprehensive counseling model
- faculty, counselor, and family collaboration
- college partnerships
- articulation

Although McDonough's college culture research does not reach below the middle school, the following section describes principles on how to create a college culture in middle and high school. In the sections that follow, discussion of the concepts includes early years and families because from day one parents play a central role in socializing and supporting students toward college.

Parent Engagement

Parent engagement in college issues begins in the early grades. Educators can engage parents in college talk so that the students receive strong messages about college throughout their school career. Perna (2002) suggests that programs targeting low-income students to facilitate educational advancement must also help parents understand the grading system. Early college awareness for parents and students includes workshop topics such as homework, good study skills, college awareness, discipline at home and school, college and university entrance requirements, along with filling out applications for scholarships to academic summer school programs, academies, and colleges.

The purpose of parent engagement is to create meaningful communication between the family and school to maximize students' learning and achievement. The most important and necessary conditions to ensure successful home/school partnerships with Latino families I call five "Cs" of parent involvement: commitment, communication, consistency, cooperation, and collaboration (Delgado Gaitan, 2004).

Commitment means that educators need to create caring and conscious change. Educators that commit to parent engagement care about changing their situation through their supportive group. Communication requires educators to reach out and listen. Listening is a two-way street. When communicating with Latino parents with limited English comprehension, educators need to communicate with parents in comprehensible language so that parents can understand their role and responsibility. While it's important for educators to impart information to parents, equally important is their ability to listen to parents about their fears, needs, questions, suggestions, and expectations. Consistency means making the process of parent involvement a continuous process, not a one-time event. Connection between educators and parents needs to be an active curriculum beginning the first day that students begin school. However, educators cannot do it alone—nor should they. Cooperation between colleagues is imperative in strengthening parent engagement. Joining with colleagues, including teachers, principals, and counselors within and between schools ensures a more cohesive relationship between parents, the community, and educators. Collaboration between educators and Latino communities enables schools to establish cultural ties between the most important institutions in students' lives. It follows that the parent partnership becomes a systematic plan, connecting the home and school. There has to be a plan in place with clear goals and strategies.

In families without college knowledge and resources, schools—through teachers and counselors—are often the only available source for advising on appropriate classes, providing basic information on why college is important, and being a sounding board for college choices. Parent workshops need to address topics ranging from online college searching to study habits and to financial preparation for college. Counselors at both the middle school and high school levels hold parent meetings throughout the year to provide information on academic and financial preparation for college.

Secondary schools typically conduct informational events about college preparedness for parents of older juniors and seniors. However, parents at all grade levels need to know how to do their part to support their children, especially Latino parents who may not have attended college. A year-end "College Fair" in Los Angeles schools that participated in McDonough's (2005) research involved students, their parents, and teachers from all grade levels in a Saturday gathering at West LA College. Colleges from across the country sent representatives to share information.

College Talk

In most middle-class families, conversations about college are commonplace. All and any talk about college qualifies as college talk. In families of Latino students, a frank and honest appraisal of what it takes to get to college requires that educators and parents create an environment where Latino student hear college talk. This requires a greater need to create an environment where talk about going to college is explicit and is heard frequently beginning in the early grades.

Some school principals conduct "college awareness" events for entire faculty and parents to emphasize the importance of strong and consistent resources on the path to college. A school fair brings in professionals from the community to speak about their work. They join a potluck and games for young children. College talk also needs to extend beyond the school to the community at large. Students have a greater need for support of their goal to get to college.

Middle schools inform students and parents about important deadlines, events, and activities such as summer academic camps through newsletters. These outlets are also used to debunk the common myths that only certain students can go to college. McDonald and Dorr (2006) describe how one Los Angeles middle school has an afternoon "College Club" where students do research on different colleges and gather information about the schools that interest them. Another strategy on the part of a middle school was to conduct an essay contest where students reflected on the question, What would you bring to college? Hundreds of submissions provided insight into students' excitement about and aspirations toward college.

Comprehensive Counseling Model

School counselors play a critical role in preparing Latino students for college. Counselors are more knowledgeable than other educators about college preparation and share college information with students with greater frequency, especially in middle and high school since teachers focus on classroom instruction. They are typically the persons responsible for fostering a college culture at the respective school. Counselors have developed an ongoing collaboration with students, parents, nonprofit organizations that encourage them to share resources and coordinate their efforts. The high school in McDonough's project has lighter counseling caseloads and all counselors are identified as college counselors.

Effective high school counselors are those who help students set clear expectations toward college by informing them about their required classes, timelines for admission applications, test schedules, and inviting university personnel to visit the school.

Faculty, Counselor, and Parent Collaboration

Counselors have major responsibilities for preparing students for college in McDonough's Los Angeles middle and high school project. They interpret test results for incorporating explanations and other materials into daily lessons. However, counselors do not do it alone. Educators have a role in creating a college culture in their respective school. Counselors create some of their own materials to provide to teachers so that they also have the opportunity to communicate a college message to their students. Faculty and counselors also need to make themselves available to families to answer any questions about students' academic future.

Martinez (2003) reported that the high school students she interviewed felt that teachers and counselors did not encourage them.

> The role of my high school teachers was minimal. I cannot recall specific examples of teachers encouraging or motivating me personally to attend an institution of higher education. My guidance counselor, for example, felt that I should not attend any four-year institution. (Javier Padilla interview, p.17)

Like Javier, many Latinos are taught that education is the key to success. By working hard, rewards will follow along with a better quality of life for the family. However, the reality is that even when students work hard, they fail to obtain the expected results. The odyssey through ineffective school systems poses preventable challenges, making it even more imperative to build a college culture from the early grades up through high school.

McDonough's research project created College Centers in four of their middle schools (McDonough, 2008). Counselors reported having students waiting outside their doors every day, eager to talk about college. At the middle school level, the counseling staff was available during homeroom periods, during lunch and nutrition, as well as before and after school. At the high school level, college centers are open throughout the day and all counselors are prepared to talk about college with the students. High school students and their parents attended presentations on financing college. College Centers at the high school level were enhanced through the identification of all counselors as college counselors.

Articulation Between Schools

Given the counselors' heavy caseloads and myriad of responsibilities, it is clear that one solitary professional cannot carry a school's college resource infrastructure. Changes must occur throughout schools so that all students hear about the college mission loud and clear. Moreover, these expectations must be present from the earliest stages of their academic career.

Systematically socializing students for college makes more sense given McDonough's (2009) assertion: Having college plans by the tenth grade increases the likelihood of attending by 21 percent compared to plans formulated during the senior year. Early plans allow students to prepare academically, financially, and even mentally. But college aspirations do not simply happen. Family and school culture needs to hold high expectations for students as part of accelerated instruction.

School counselors directly reach students as early as fifth grade. In the schools involved in McDonough's project, the counseling process has begun to be more fluid, with greater integration of guidance counseling across all levels. High school and middle school counseling staffs are relying on each other to a greater degree and pooling resources to increase the impact of their work.

College Partnerships

Counselors involved with the McDonough's College Talk project in the middle and secondary schools have organized numerous trips to college campuses around the Los Angeles area. Through these trips, students gain a greater understanding of what college life is like. When they talk about college in the classroom, they now have a vivid picture of it.

All of the schools in the Los Angeles research project (McDonough, 2005) held events such as College Week, College Night, or Career Week to emphasize the importance of higher education. These events included guest speakers, college dress days, door decoration contests, and other activities designed to expose students to a range of college options.

Several schools established and expanded tutoring programs that connect college students with high school and middle school students. These programs not only helped students academically but also exposed them to college and students who share backgrounds similar to their own. Middle school students participated in a pen pal program that allowed them to communicate with college students with similar backgrounds and experiences.

REFLECTIONS

From kindergarten through high school, career days, college visits, and mentoring programs underlie a strong college culture by preparing Latino students for college. Key features of a successful college culture involve maintaining the idea of college forefront in students' minds throughout all grades, providing students with comprehensive counseling, preparing teachers to deal with all the needed knowledge and strategies, as well as collaboration among students, educators, and families.

While the possibilities are many for implementing educational pillars to socialize Latinos for college and place them on the right course, educators cannot dismiss the bigger systemic picture of restructuring education to eliminate injustices in the educational system, particularly tracking students according to expectations. Financing schools equitably and preparing teachers for a diverse population constitute part of the major policies to re-create. Since schools are part of the larger society in this world economy that requires an educated, professional workforce, education is top priority. And so is the family system that undergirds students' educational foundation. For that reason, we cannot ignore the fact that the issue of getting Latinos to college extends beyond the school doors. Families, too, must have adequate employment, housing, and a meaningful position in their community, enabling them to enhance the support for their children's education.

Talking College in Elementary School

4

COLLEGE TALK IN THE FIRST GRADE

Señora (Mrs.) Eva lives with her son and 8-year-old granddaughter, Blanca. For the most part, she takes charge of the home front, which includes Blanca's schooling in a large urban school district. She meets with teachers and stays informed on Blanca's educational needs, including homework and meeting with her teacher.

(Translated from Spanish) I didn't have the opportunity to go to school in Mexico, but when my son and I immigrated here, I wanted him to take advantage of educational opportunities. I always reminded him to do his homework and I talked with his teachers as much as possible so I could help him in whatever way I could. But, for as much as I did, he decided not to go to college. He said he was very bored with school. He just started working and that ended his schooling. Then when Blanca was born, I saw my role as one of helping her and keeping her interested in school, especially because my son worked long hours. When Blanca began first grade, the teacher said that she needed more practice with reading. So, at nights I sat with her and read some of her favorite storybooks along with the ones that the teacher sent home. During our times together I also talked with her about how important it was for her to love learning everything she could in school so that she could go to college after high school and get a wonderful job that paid lots of money for her. I reminded her that she was very smart and she would keep getting smarter every day, the more she read and learned.

I loved walking her to school because I went into her classroom and got to see how Mr. Fuentes put up all the students' writing and pictures for all the students' to admire. They all got to see each other's work and I liked that. One of the things that I loved most about Mr. Fuentes was that he had a chart up on the front board. It had a list of instructions to remind the children about what was important in life. It read:

- Work carefully
- Eat healthy
- Have good role models that teach you
- Have confidence in yourself
- Plan to go to college
- Love learning as much as you can about everything

To me this list says that he holds important high expectations for his students. He respects them and he believes that they should do their best. Mr. Fuentes was a bilingual teacher. When I told him that I appreciated that he cared so much about his students' learning, he told me that he felt a big responsibility for them because most of the students in the class were Latinos. And many Latinos don't go to college. I was so impressed that a first-grade teacher would be preparing his young students to look into their future and think about how much they're capable of learning. I think about it all the time and remind my little Blanca how important everything on that list is so she will get into college.

Effective educators like Mr. Fuentes set high academic expectations for Latino students. A critically important program for English learners is bilingual education. Successful programs contribute to their academic achievement of English learners. Decades of bilingual education debates highlight the unsettled theoretical and philosophical issues of bilingual instruction in the educational system. The most complete research on the topic has determined the importance of language programs in English and the students' home language (Collier & Thomas, 2009; Greene, 1998). Since the 1960s, various models and types of programs have been practiced. The dual-language approach develops both English and the students' home language since both are used to teach subject matters. The program reveals the best academic results, strengthens cultural identities, and affirms social justice for the language group. The value has been evidenced in achievement gains of up to fifteen percentile points in math and reading compared with students who receive instruction in English only. Bilingual programs enhance students' self-confidence by valuing the students' culture, improving acquisition and retention of new knowledge, and facilitating literacy and learning subject matter for English learners.

The most important relationships in children's academic lives are adults in the school and home setting. In the vignettes that follow, students share about the role that adults play in moving them along the college path through discipline, hard work, and revealing their dreams and their plans.

SUPPORTIVE RELATIONSHIPS IN THE SCHOOL SETTING

The classroom is the educational setting and teachers are the most critical players in the learning process since they work with students several hours daily. When teachers create meaningful classroom instruction through advanced verbal interaction between students and teachers, students' learning increases compared to settings where teachers direct the instruction and minimize student engagement. This requires dynamic leadership at the school and district level to support teachers in developing instructional programs that maximize students' language, culture, and learning potential (Gonzalez, 2009). Teachers that students remember most respect students' culture, encourage their full potential, engage parents and community members, and challenge students through rigorous programmatic curriculum designs for students from underrepresented immigrant groups that often find themselves in a high risk academically.

Teachers who encourage language through stories about professionals in different fields help students envision future careers. "Talk explicitly about the importance of going to college even if it seems difficult. Don't deny the world your gifts," says Debra, a second-grade teacher, "You all have wonderful talents to develop. Give yourself every opportunity." She laughed, recounting that one student raised his hand and said, "But I can't go to college. I don't even know how to read and write very well." Debra reassured him that he would know how to read and write very well by the time he was of age to enter college.

A critical way of promoting a college-bound commitment is by creating enduring home and school partnerships. Schools that utilize the families' cultural strengths and knowledge about their children improve students' achievement (Delgado Gaitan, 2001, 2004).

It may seem common knowledge to most people that succeeding academically means regular attendance. Yet when it comes to building a college culture for Latino students, the message needs to be stronger in some schools. Absenteeism may be an issue in schools with high Latino student enrollment. In elementary grades, parents sometimes keep young children home when they have medical appointments so they can help care for babies in the family. Parents need ways to rethink their family dilemmas that sometimes contribute to student absenteeism. Students may convince their parents that they're not feeling well to stay home when in fact the only problem is that they're not doing well in school and fear more failure when they attend. In meetings with parents as well as in weekly newsletters to families, schools need to reinforce the importance of getting their children to school every day.

In one semirural school where most of the enrollment was Latino, educators found themselves at a loss to figure out how to maintain regular attendance. Sherrie, a third-grade teacher, tells her story of the frustration she felt in maintaining regular attendance until she convinced her colleagues to work with her.

Sherrie impressed upon her colleagues of the importance of student attendance. She knew that teachers needed to keep students interested in school in order to get them engaged. Although the program she worked with in her former school had been successful, she couldn't organize it alone. She convinced her colleagues of this very important concept of student daily attendance and described some of the weekly activities that the girls did at the campuses. The classrooms competed for perfect attendance by spelling and they succeeded in reaching 100 percent attendance everyday in most classrooms. To involve the community, student participants took the grade-level information and made charts for the school so they could discuss daily attendance with their parents present. Parents and students collaborated on this project. Teachers acknowledged their achievements. Parents were invited because they had a lot to do with motivating students. Students talked about attendance. The school put the attendance message on their electronic board in the front of the school: *"Learning makes us better people, come to school every day* (Vengan a las escuela todos los dias porque cada dia aprendemos ser mejores personas)." Weekly, the principal called parents through the electronic phone system. The power of collaboration with parents played out gradually as student attendance improved at Sherrie's new school.

Teacher Connecting With Students

Students' early dreams mean a great deal in shaping self-esteem, motivation, and inspiration. Teachers play an important role in helping students direct and take practical steps toward making their dreams a reality. Monica attends an urban area elementary school, which has a high Latino enrollment. She wants to be an anesthesiologist. In the fifth grade, she read many books about doctors and the different fields of medicine available for specialization.

When I first decided what I wanted to be, I chose being an anesthesiologist. That is a person that puts people to sleep before an operation. By being a doctor, I can help people get better. I like to help other people because I don't like to see them sick or to see them with any kind of diseases. After my teacher invited a doctor to visit our classroom and talk to us about his career, she helped me to research what an anesthesiologist is paid. They get paid more than other doctors. This is what made me change my mind. Right now, I help my mom when my sisters get sick. This makes me feel helpful and I am doing something for someone else. I want to help the people when they need an operation. It is going to take a long time, but I am willing to go to college to take all the classes that I need after high school. I'm just in the sixth grade, but I plan to hang in there and get to college and study every day. My teacher tells me that I have to take lots of chemistry and math classes. I'm pretty sure that I can do well because I have good grades in my math. I hope that I am going to do well in chemistry and other sciences in high school. I think that it is very hard being an anesthesiologist because you can kill patients if you put too much or very little medicine make them to sleep. You should also be very dedicated to your work and I know that I am very dedicated. I think that you must do your work very well so that you can get paid well.

Monica's informed career goal, in the sixth grade, to become an anesthesiologist speaks volumes about the supportive educational environment she has because, for too long, young Latino students have held lofty dreams about professional careers without understanding the pragmatic steps to reach those goals through college. Monica's teacher is preparing her students to think about their careers by considering the concrete steps to reaching those goals, including hard work, long-range planning and perseverance.

Early Mentoring

Mentors play important roles at every age of the students' schooling. Angelina was a second-grade student and Sandra was a high school senior who volunteered as a mentor at the local elementary school. One Saturday, she took Angelina with her to visit a college. It was an annual event where college students oriented high school students about campus life. Sandra asked her parents and her teacher for permission to take Angelina. Her parents wondered why it was important for a second grader to visit a college. Sandra explained to them,

I've been helping Angelina with her math and English. She is a very smart little girl and I want her to know that she should start thinking about going to college. When I was her age, I didn't have anyone to tell me about college until now that I'm in high school. If I had known about college, I would have loved making plans about where I was going to go and what I was going to study for my career.

The college visit was a special event for Angelina. They visited the library and other places, including the bookstore. They had lunch at the student union, which Angelina enjoyed. She was impressed with how big the college was. At the end of the day, Sandra said that the visit answered the question, How is it being in a college for the first time? Angelina said that it was like being at *a great big school*. Sandra felt that Angelina had a greater opportunity to imagine realistic career plans with a focus on college.

Another example of mentoring young girls comes from a program for mothers and daughters in northern California. The county office–led Mother/Daughter (M/D) program organized fourth-and fifth-grade girls from several schools. The girls had to make a two-year commitment to attend academic tutoring classes twice weekly after school with their mothers. They attended weekly literacy meetings, worked with a community mentor, and attended quarterly career fairs and biannual college visits. When girls began the M/D program, they and the moms were often uninformed, uncertain, or undecided about their career. They did not know how to make career choices. The mothers met weekly to share their personal stories about their supporting their daughters' schooling. After talking about their experiences, they wrote down their stories. At the same time that the moms met, the girls met with one of the organizers. They also discussed their school experiences and wrote about their college plans. The girls shared their written stories with each other.

Maria's story is a common one in the initial phase of college knowledge, until they got better informed and comfortable with what the college experience meant.

I don't want to live away from home, so I want to go to a college that is nearby. The thing is that my mother needs help with my brothers and sisters. At first, I didn't think that I wanted to go to college, but since my mother and I started coming to the M/D program, I think I understand what it is. My mother talks to me about my schoolwork and even about my plans for what kind of career I want to study when I go to college. So, I'll need to go to a nearby college. There are a few of them around here. We have some choices.

Drawing on the personal experience with her family, Maria looks forward with an understanding of what it takes to be an independent woman. Her ability to plan a lifestyle to support independence while maintaining her family ties speaks to what she will have to consider as she sets forth to live apart from her family while educating herself.

Elementary school mentor programs and career fairs in a rather remote school in a rural part of Texas helped Latino students improve their academic potential and acquaint them with the necessary competencies for college. The school principal collaborated with the county migrant program to bring in academic mentors and career fairs.

Fourth grader Mona helped her mother translate at the local health clinic where the nurses spoke some Spanish but not the doctors who worked there part time. She had her eyes on a career as a doctor, but at this point, her academic work needed much improvement.

I want to be a doctor because I like to help people and I like to work with little kids. I don't like to see people suffer. I am going to do everything that's in my hands to help my community that's very poor. I am going to help my community by doing my best to cure the people and try to keep them alive. Being a doctor is also going to help me, because I would understand other people's conditions and I am going to be able to provide all that my family needs. To get to my goal, I've learned that I need to work hard on my school-work. For example, I need to do my homework and turn it in on time. I also have to try not to get in trouble. Bertha, my mentor at school, is helping me a lot. She tutors me and I'm learning how to do math and to read better. And my grades have improved. She also tells me that I need to spend more time studying not only what the teacher assigns for homework, but I should read lots of other books and stories. That way I can learn to become a doctor when I grow up. If I don't get good grades, I won't be able to go to college. Nothing is going to stop me from achieving my goal. And, thanks to Bertha, I have learned to never give up and always do my best even when it's difficult so I can make my dream happen, no matter what.

Mona illustrates the importance of students' understanding the value of good study habits in getting good grades in early years. Persevering through hard work is in her plans because she feels able to rely on Bertha, her mentor. In the fourth grade, Mona sees lot of possibilities opening up for her because she has improved her grades through good study skills.

After-School Activities

Neighborhood social contexts influence how Latino students may be hindered or succeed in their pursuit of college (Garcia-Reid & Peterson, 2005; Vasquez, 2007). A neighborhood between Jamaica Plain and Roxbury in the Boston area is a community known as the cocaine capital of the area. In this environment, Hyde Square Task Force (HSTF), a non-profit community organization, has worked tirelessly, partnering with elementary, middle, and high schools as well as community organizations and local colleges to support students in their academic pursuits since 1980 (Hyde Square Task Force, 2012).

A graduate of HSTF programs, Catalina shares her elementary school experience in the after-school program at Kennedy School. When she was in the third grade, tutors from HSTF came to her school to start a tutoring program. Catalina tells how the after-school program answered her needs.

Our school was mostly Puerto Rican and Dominican Republic. The Hyde Square Task Force offered tutoring for everyone who wanted to attend. I wanted to learn English and needed help with my homework because my parents only spoke Spanish. They were very supportive about me getting a good education because my mother was a teacher. I had a few friends in the school and they went to the after-school program, so I wanted to be there too. I didn't want to become like other kids that were always getting into trouble with early pregnancies, drugs, gangs and lots of gun violence in the streets. It's a bit better now, but it was quite bad when I was growing up here.

Most of the time they tutored us and we did our homework. One day a week we got to go work with a dance group, Ritmo in Acción. And on another day, a Youth Literacy tutor came to read books to the kids. My parents gave me permission to stay after school because the gym where we were tutored was very close to the school. But it was easy for my mother to come to pick me up

because we lived half a block away. It's not the kind of neighborhood where kids should walk alone.

All through school I watched girls I knew get pregnant and
get into other trouble and never finish school. Then when I got
to high school, the Hyde Square Task Force found me a mentor.
She was a lawyer. She was great. In fact, I still have contact with
her even now that I've graduated from college. I thank her for
guiding me through the college application process and taking
me to tour colleges. I learned so much from her about college
and how to become a lawyer. In my junior year in high school, I
needed a job and Hyde Square hired me as a tutor. As it turned
out I went to Suffolk University, but I majored in Sociology.
Throughout my college years, I worked in Hyde Square, and in
my senior year I became a coordinator of the same after-school
tutoring program that got me started in the third grade. Now,
I'm getting ready to go to Boston University for my master's in
social work.

What began as a small community service organization, HSTF has
expanded to where it is currently serving 1,000 students ages 6–21
through educational, health, arts programs, and organizing community
events. HSTF is proud of their record for getting young Latinos from their
community to college. Catalina's successful and supportive path toward
college is one of many students from these local neighborhoods that credit
HSTF for their success in college. HSTF reports that since 2003, 100 percent of HSTF's youth leaders have enrolled in college and 80 percent have
graduated within 5 years (Hyde Square Task Force, 2012).

BUILDING COLLEGE CULTURE
RELATIONSHIPS BETWEEN FAMILY AND SCHOOL

Although schools attempt to provide tutors and mentors for students,
professional role models for Latino students may be scarce in working-
class communities, where few adults graduate from college. In such cases,
community-at-large role models are important in socializing young Latino
students for college. Through such local programs as the Tecnología y la
Familia (Technology and the Family), Latino parents become inspired to
learn and in turn, they inspire students and other parents to pursue college.
For example, Lorena was a Costa Rican immigrant with one daughter in
elementary school, Raquel, and another one in high school, Laura. Lorena,

worked as a custodian at her local high school. She became involved in the *Tecnología y la Familia* when her younger daughter was in fourth grade. Initially in the Saturday mother groups, Lorena was quite shy about sharing her immigrant experience with others. However, in her written statements, she expressed her heartfelt desire for her girls to get the best education possible and break the cycle of poverty and abuse that she experienced. The more she participated in the program, the more she became involved in her daughters' schooling and grew to be a strong advocate for her girls. Lorena's confidence also grew to where she volunteered to lead training meetings for the moms to learn to communicate with school personnel as well as learn how to provide their children with the information and encouragement to plan for college beginning in the elementary school years. Parents felt grateful for the inspiration she extended to them.

With the director's assistance, Lorena learned to prepare meetings, communicate clearly, and inform the group of parents on strategies for supporting their children in their education and to locate community resources to accelerate their children's academic standing. As she assumed the leadership role, other moms admired her and felt convinced of their own ability to lead. Gradually, she convinced other moms to step up and learn how to assist others and lead parent training. Laura was most appreciative of her advocacy as she learned about a math enrichment camp during the summer at Stanford University for high school students. She and Laura solicited the high school counselor's assistance and that of the *Tecnología y la Familia* program director to complete the application. All along, Lorena took Raquel along so that she could learn the various steps to obtain services and resources improve her academic opportunities. Laura submitted the application and waited anxiously until the good-news envelope arrived in her mail. She credited her mother's involvement in her schooling for helping her obtain important educational rewards. Lorena's own education and employment also expanded. She earned a General Education Diploma (GED), went to the community college, and trained in business. Within a year, she obtained a secretarial position in an elementary school.

Identifying Talents Early

Reading and writing came easy for Paula in the sixth grade. However, because she was a good student, educators often assumed that she could carve out her own path to college. Fortunately, Mrs. Cortez, Paula's teacher, recognized her interest and talent and cultivated it through the curriculum. The teacher made them write many stories about their family as well as fiction. For Paula, there was no greater challenge or love.

My mother read to me a lot when I was a little girl. Then I started reading to my little brother and sister. Since then, I knew I wanted to be a writer. I liked telling stories. When I read to my sister and brother, I read from the book, but sometimes I liked pretending that I was reading and making up my own story. Then I started making up stories and writing them down. But it wasn't until the sixth grade with Mrs. Cortez that I really got to write. She made us write and write and write. She said that in middle school, we would have to do lot of writing. She taught us to write about our families and then to make up fictional characters and plots. I made up lot of weird characters because I enjoy making people laugh. I want to be a writer because I love to write short stories that are funny. When I get to high school, I would like to take a creative writing class. Then, I would like to go to college and get a degree in writing. That seems like a long time away, but there's a lot I have to learn before that. Then, I would like to start a short children's book and work my way up to a big novel-type book. My teacher, Mrs. Cortez, and my mother, too, have really helped me to get excited about learning about careers like a writer's career and finding what is good for me. I got to go to visit a college a few months ago and talk with students who are taking writing classes. That was a dream come true. It was like I could picture myself being there. When I write I feel like I'm in a whole different world. For some of my friends, writing is very difficult. But for me it is the easiest thing ever. No matter what people say, I'm going to keep on writing because it is my dream. To other people, writing is not important, but sometimes people need to read stories that are interesting to help them get to imagine how it was when they were kids. Writing is very important to me and I am never going to stop.

Paula's teacher, Mrs. Cortez, held high expectations for her and in a concrete way made Paula understand that it wasn't enough to have an interest in writing. She had to work hard to succeed in her craft. Her enthusiasm for pursuing and working hard to accomplish her dream puts her on the college track.

Planning Realistically

In a small suburban school, students from second through sixth grade who apply receive tutoring and mentoring after school with teacher recommendation. Most of them are Latino students with academic needs. Danny works with mentors to improve his math and literacy skills. He is a third grader who wants to become a veterinarian.

I knew I wanted to be a vet since I was very little. We had a dog and we used to take him to get shots at the vet. So, I want to be a vet because I love animals, but the only way I can get there is by going to school. But just attending class isn't enough. I have to get good grades, pass all my tests, and go to college. Plus, I have to have fun. Being a vet would be the greatest thing ever! I would be able to make a difference in the world. I love to have and to help animals. All kinds. I would never hit an animal, even if it bit me, because they're probably just scared. You can't blame them. College is important because I need to know where everything in their body is so I don't kill them. Work hard is what I have to do if I want to get a degree and start my own business, like a vet clinic. I better get busy!

Education is the key! I have to do well in school so I can get to college. I need to pay attention in class right now. Then when I get to college, I can learn new things. Learning is very important also because I have to learn where everything is in the animal's body. I need to get a degree so I can prove I learned while I was in school. I have to get good grades. I can't rush through my homework or I might get wrong answers. If I don't turn in my paper at all I am going to get a zero. That's really bad! I'll have to go to field trips to vet hospitals and I should read a lot of books about pet care. I know how to take care of our dog, but I need to learn how to care for other animals. And that means going to college. I also have to attend school without being absent because I'll miss lessons. I just have to keep working hard!

Danny's work with mentors moves him forward to connect the importance of day-to-day behaviors such as hard work, good grades, and daily attendance in his current grade level. He is learning the importance of continuing these good habits throughout his schooling that increases his potential to achieve his goal of succeeding in his college and becoming a vet.

Learning Confidence

Celia credits the key adults in her life—parents, teachers, and mentors—who enable her to face her academic challenges and not shy away from difficult work. It is a critical skill throughout school.

I'm not really sure what exactly I want to be in the future, but right now I feel like becoming a children's psychologist. It will be kind of hard because of all the schooling I'll have to go through, but if I set my mind to it, I know I can do it. I have learned how to have confidence in myself. My parents, teachers, and mentors here in school teach me that even when things are hard, I need to do them. And, you know, when I do that, I feel better—not afraid. I like being in the after-school mentor project that the principal began because the mentors here have helped me to get good grades. I did OK before, but now I get better grades. My mentor, Yoli, is in college and tells me all about college and how I can get there so I can become a psychologist or whatever I want to be. Right now, I would like becoming a psychologist because I like to make people feel happy. I also like to help people with their problems. To get my goal I know for sure that I will need to graduate from high school with a diploma. After that, I will have to go to college and major in psychology. To graduate from college, it will probably take me at least four years. After this, I can keep going to college to get higher degrees. The more education I have, the more money I will be able to earn. I should do well because I'm really interested and I will have fun studying psychology. Right now, I have to make sure that I listen in class and try not to fail any tests. Once I get into middle and high school, I have to keep getting good grades all the way to college. By doing this, I can get a scholarship to pay for my college tuition. Right now all I have to do is focus my mind to my goals and not listen to anyone who may try to put me down by calling me a nerd for getting good grades. I still don't know how I will pay for my college education. I can probably work at a restaurant to start saving money for college. Of course, I can't get a job right now until the first summer in high school. I'm always bored at home during the summers anyway. I'm going to do my best. I will keep learning how to be a responsible person and have confidence to do my work. I really hope I can reach my goals! Oh, by the way, in the future when you have problems remember to come to me! I'll be able to take care of people with problems.

Celia's story illustrates the significance of collaboration between parents, educators, and mentors in focusing students toward college. With their support and instruction, Celia's grades improved. This gives her the confidence to move forward even if she doesn't have all the answers she needs.

The concept of self-esteem may seem very vague and abstract to young students, but it matters a great deal in academic achievement. However, in many Latino families, children are held to high standards in their behavior. Among them, respect for self and others as well as cooperation.

Values Shape Dreams

Third grader Omar describes what his parents taught him about self-respect and its importance where his educational future is concerned. With his eyes set on law, Omar is already putting his plan in action.

My parents and grandparents, who live with us, always tell me to have respect for myself and other people. I think that if I respect myself, I am doing the right thing. How I stay true to myself is that I keep my goals and dreams realistic and try my hardest all the time. And, if for some reason something goes wrong at school, I try to do my best and get it right the next time. My parents want me to go to college even if they couldn't go. So, I can help myself by boosting my self-esteem and reminding myself that achieving my goals and dreams would make me feel really happy. And, if I could do that, I would feel that I have good self-respect. To be a lawyer, I'll need more school, like college. And, I'll need good grades to get to college. My parents help with that, like with homework and when I don't know something they help me find a way to learn it. It's like your inner self telling you, 'You can do it.' To make all my dreams and goals come true I need to have dedication and ambition, to accomplish this I will work hard.

Respect is often an attribute describing Latino families. Many Latino adults expect their children to be respectful as in Omar's family. Third grader Omar internalizes a sense of self-respect by being a good student. His story illustrates the parents' influence on Latino students' academic work even if they themselves have not had a formal education. This acknowledges the importance of educators to communicate meaningfully with Latino parents.

REFLECTIONS

College talk in the elementary level points to the power of personal relationships with significant adults. Such relationships are attainable to students who have teachers, parents, and mentors. This means that everyone needs to become a mentor for young Latino students, including high school and college students, professionals, and leaders in the community. These personal contacts provide the subtle and explicit messages that are important as well as guiding and challenging students to keep growing and learning.

Some of the stories tell how elementary school students are self-reliant and work independently to orient themselves through school. But even in such cases, students need the continual supportive encouragement of educators in their daily school life and a warm word from a loving and caring parent. Knowledge drives the changes that students need to make in order to plan for college appropriately. Informed students and parents can advocate for themselves. Regardless of how self-directed some students may be, a strong college culture in elementary schools is important in order to serve all students in school as well as the community. The stories in this chapter provide a window into the strength of school and family relationships that guide elementary-level students toward college awareness, academic preparedness, and hopeful visions, making home/ school partnerships a critical component in building a college culture.

PRACTICAL STRATEGIES FOR ELEMENTARY-GRADE EDUCATORS

Message From Students' Personal Stories on Building College-Bound Potential

- In their different roles, educators, parents, and community professionals guide Latino students through their academic school experience and inspire them to work hard toward their college-bound goals.
- Educators motivate students to pursue a college direction by moving them closer to their dreams through challenging curriculum and constant encouragement.
- School mentors inform students about college by helping them create long-term goals.
- Learning from meaningful and trusting mentorship relationships helps make future career interests a practical reality.
- Early local college socialization programs such as the Mother and Daughter program help create a college culture by providing mentors, tutors, college visits, and parent engagement to assist students in career planning and college awareness.
- Latino families value respect of others and of oneself. Children learn self-respect through academic performance and use it as an avenue to climb the ladder to college.

Idea

Mentors in elementary schools provide an important service by informing students on the specifics of getting to college. How elementary schools can organize a mentor program with high schools take many forms, depending on the resources and available mentors outside of the school. However, what they all have in common is the value that they provide for orienting students toward college.

Suggestion for Instruction

Teachers can share their own story with students and have students write about what they think college is and how will it help them reach their goals.

Planning Effective School Site Mentoring Program

Organizing effective mentor programs in elementary schools can take many forms. However, some points need to be considered when serving Latino students:

- Defining. Program goals for underachieving students.
- Recruiting. High school and college students, community professionals, and leaders, retired adults, community groups such as Big Brothers/Big Sisters serve as mentors (since more females volunteer, make an effort to recruit minority males for boys).
- Referring. Educators and parents request and refer students for mentoring.
- Duration. Dyads last for the duration of a school year (possibly during the summer).
- Matching. Shared interests, skills, and strengths match up students and mentors.
- Mentoring. Incorporate structured tutoring and unstructured activities.
- Orienting. Provide preorientation for mentor and student as well as ongoing training during the year.
- Collecting information. Provide mentors, students, and teachers a checklist to track activities.
- Evaluating. The success of the program is about development of a trusting and mutually satisfying relationship that improves attendance and performance.

College Readiness in Middle and Secondary School

5

During middle and secondary years, students confront major emotional and social challenges while they navigate increasingly more difficult academic material. An academically good middle school student, Anita, gives a glimpse of how arrangements between schools and families support her through family crisis that might otherwise have disadvantaged her overall progress.

I was in middle school when my grandparents came to live with Mom and me because my grandmother was very ill. My aunts and uncles helped, but Mom's a nurse so she did lot of the care. I don't know why, but I got kinda upset when my room was taken over and I had to sleep in the living room. So I thought that she didn't care about me, especially because she spent most of her time taking care of my grandparents. I tried to do my homework in the living room or kitchen, but there was always something happening and I wasn't comfortable. So one day at school, I didn't do my homework right and the teacher called on me and I didn't know the answer. One boy that didn't like me started teasing me and I threw a pencil at him and got in trouble. It didn't stop there. That same kid kept teasing me about being fat and how Mexicans were fat. I told the teacher, but she just told the kid to stop it. I told Mom and she went talk to the teacher to tell her how this kid was bothering me, but the teacher just complained to Mom about the homework that I wasn't doing right and that I was misbehaving in class.

Mom asked my aunts and uncles to help me with my homework, so they took turns helping me. They helped me a lot because I didn't feel like I was so alone. One of my uncles took me to

57

school one day and talked with my teacher to see if the school could help me to find a tutor. The teacher told the principal and he helped put me in a program for tutoring and mentoring students who don't get good grades. At first I didn't want to go because I told my uncle that I always got good grades. He told me that it would be good for me to try it for a while. So I did. I liked it right away because the girl, Sandra, that tutored me was very nice and she went to high school. She told me all about it. I didn't feel so scared about high school after talking with her. When she saw that my math and science grades improved, she invited me to visit the high school. That was so much fun. Sandra kept tutoring me and I knew I could get into the advanced classes like I wanted to. She actually did more than that, she mentored me and guided me on how to be a good student in high school. Too bad she graduated just as I got started.

I think Sandra helped me so much that I knew what to do in high school. I knew I had to work harder than in middle school and she showed me what I had to do to study so I did well in all my classes, even math and science. Mom was very proud of me. She didn't worry so much about me because I felt more confident and I wanted to go to school and I could figure out how to ask for help. Even after I got into college, I stayed in touch with Sandra.

Anita's safety nets, her family and the tutor/mentor that the school provided, helped her get back on track and gave her the confidence she needed to move forward into high school. She learned how to access the necessary support resources to get into advanced classes.

By middle school, Latino students need to have a strong academic, social, and emotional support system that serves as a catalyst and a safety net. These program features frame the general topics in this chapter.

Many tutoring/mentoring programs such as Anita's school provided may be considered remediation because they operate on basis that students lack academic skills. Although students benefit from the additional support, some schools have adopted a different model, a program of a more empowering nature.

Middle school raises the stakes for students in preparation for college. Academic performance matters more than ever. Researchers (Engle, Bermeo, & O'Brian, 2006; Cavazos, & Cavazos, 2010) recognize five major educational features that promote strong academic success for Latino students as expectations increase in middle school and further increase in high school:

- Tutoring and mentoring
- Preparing for advanced courses
- Developing good study habits and skills
- Establish sustained parent/school partnerships
- Ensuring supportive academic transition from middle through high school

ADVANCED COURSES

Traditionally, schools address the problem of student preparation for advanced courses by restricting enrollment in those courses to the best-prepared students. This approach leads to the typical outcome that only a select few students take advanced courses. This impedes the goal of preparing underrepresented students for college. It also does not encourage students to take on a more interesting high school curriculum.

After leaving high school in a small suburban town, Ramon reflected on his career goal to become an architect and how he was fortunate to have two excellent teachers who took an interest in him and steered him in the right direction.

Getting through advanced classes: "From the beginning in elementary school, I liked school and enjoyed working hard to get good grades. Although I did not know what college was or that I needed to go there, I knew that I was willing to work hard to learn everything I needed to know. So, I did that until about the sixth grade when I started having problems with math. My teacher was not very supportive. He just kept telling me that I wasn't working hard enough and that's why I couldn't do the work. I kept asking him to help me, but then he told me to go ask someone else because he wouldn't help a lazy student. I tried telling my parents, but they just kept telling me to try harder because they didn't know how to help me. A neighbor told them that I should get a tutor, but my dad said that he didn't have the money for that. I felt too embarrassed to tell my friends or to ask someone else in the school for help. It just kept going that way and I got a 'D' grade in math."

When I got to middle school, they wouldn't let me take algebra because I had a low grade before, so they made me take "pre-algebra." I still had a problem understanding the stuff. I asked the teacher to help me after school or before school. I didn't care when I had to show up, I really just wanted to "get it."

Mr. Suarez said that he'd help me after school because he thought I really cared about learning the stuff. The first thing he asked me was, What do you want to be when you grow up? I told him that I wanted to be an architect. He got very excited and said that I needed to know all the math, algebra, geometry, and all the higher math through high school so I could get into college and do well in my major. I didn't know that, but once he told me that I got excited and I felt that I would be able to learn whatever math I had to learn to become an architect.

After I left Mr. Suarez's class, he kept calling me into his classroom and asking me how my algebra class was going. It wasn't easy, and at one point I told him that I was running into trouble again. He asked me who was helping me. I said that sometimes the algebra teacher tried to help me when she had time, but there were too many students. Mr. Suarez said that if I could come to his classroom early mornings before class, he'd help me. He was so great to do that, so I accepted. I'd show up mornings and he helped me. Without him, I wouldn't have made it through middle school.

Then high school was another trip. They made me take algebra again, because they said my grades weren't good enough. I didn't mind it because at least I did very well. Then came geometry one and two. I liked them better, but still needed help and sometimes I could see a tutor that came to the school after school. But, it was not as often as I needed it. This time I went to Mr. Suarez at the middle school that was not too far from the high school. I told him that I really needed help and wondered how he might be able to help me. As always, he was very helpful and told me that he could do it after-school and Saturday mornings at the library.

Ramon's story spotlights the difficulty that many Latino students face in being underprepared for advanced high school classes. Some issues with enrolling Latino students in advanced placement courses involve the lack of academic preparation they need to succeed in those classes. Enrolling students in courses without making a systematic effort to get them ready and giving them course credit even if they don't learn the content implied by the course title is not working well either. An analogy can be drawn to the debate over social promotion. Giving students credit for courses for which they haven't learned the content is like socially promoting a student who is unprepared for the next grade. But excluding students from advanced courses—such as retaining the student in the previous grade without offering appropriate interventions—does not seem to work well either. As is the case with policies for promoting students, there are no easy solutions.

Since the 1983 Nation at Risk report, which focused on failing schools in the United States, a major strategy for increasing students' college readiness has been to enroll more underrepresented students in advanced and college-preparatory courses in high school. The goal is to encourage college-bound students to take four years of English and at least three years of each, math, science and social studies. According to Dougherty, Mellor, and Jian (2006) at the National Center for Educational Accountability, some schools are preparing students to enter advanced classes by approaching the problem of underrepresentation in a more systematically supportive way. Students who enter high school with major deficiencies in prerequisite skills to succeed in advanced classes pose a staggering charge to educators. Interventions need to happen early so that as many students as possible enter high school with the prerequisite skills they will need to succeed in advanced courses. Ensuring that advanced courses truly prepare all students is the subject of a report by the National Center for Educational Accountability.

Workable remedies focus on most or all of the following elements:

- Higher performing schools and districts are more likely to use exams to monitor whether the system of increasing enrollment in advanced placement classes is working effectively to help students of all socioeconomic backgrounds learn the content in their advanced courses. For example, Garden Grove, California has developed end-of-course exams in 10 courses not tested by the state. Long Beach School District has developed similar exams in 43 courses from eighth grade through high school.

- A common practice in higher performing middle schools is the early identification of each student's missing prerequisite skills necessary for advanced placement classes. In those schools, teachers keep close tabs on each student's course-relevant skills and share that information as needed with the student's other teachers.

- High-performing schools and districts are more likely to use programs and strategies that help create a "culture of achievement" among their students. These include awarding letters for academic achievement, promotion of academic achievement through students' extracurricular activities, and adoption of programs that promote higher student aspirations.

- Educators collectivize in problem-solving teams to identify students with academic difficulty and to assess the necessary skills and concepts they need. Higher performing schools and districts are also more likely to use interim exams given during the course. Rather than simply pushing struggling students out of the courses, they are more likely to develop strategies to help them. These districts are more likely to organize educators into problem-solving collectives, ensuring that those educators have the information and resources they need to address students' problems.

- Teacher development is critical. In higher performing schools and districts, even teachers who are highly knowledgeable about the subject matter they are teaching require constant updating. They receive development funds to assist them in working with students who need more carefully designed instruction and extra help in order to master advanced material.

English, math, and science are particularly important courses for students in middle school since they need to establish a strong basis to enter advanced classes. Unfortunately, many Latino students are relegated to English learner classes and remain there if they have not developed their English skills sufficiently to compete in advanced classes. This makes tutors and mentors indispensible.

DEVELOPING STUDY HABITS
AND ACADEMIC LANGUAGE

Although study skills need to be taught as early as elementary school, they become paramount in the middle school grades. Classwork becomes more complex and abstract, requiring students to think more analytically and critically than in earlier grades. Before getting to high school, for Latino students, developing study skills means explicit instruction on what it means to build such skills as discipline, time organization, and preparing for tests. For many, good study habits are foreign territory because, unless they have had strong academic preparation, they may believe that succeeding or failing in schoolwork is dependent on personal luck. Key college readiness academic language and study skills include asking questions in class, budgeting time, mind games, working in study groups, and learning academic language.

Inquiry and study skills are part of the intellectual, academic package for students. Students need to learn how to ask critical questions during class time so that they access the maximum information and fully comprehend the subject. Educators need to design learning activities that actively engage students to become independent learners.

Learning Academic Language

Academic language plays a pivotal role in classroom instruction and learning in all content areas such as reading, writing, and discussion. Students, whether they are English native speakers or English language learners (ELL), need to be able to understand and use the language of all the subject content. Just hearing language in the classroom is insufficient to ensure proficiency according to Fisher and Frey (2011) and Zwiers (2007). Academic language is critical to advance students' academic achievement and prepare them for college. Academic language instruction needs to be explicit to the extent of making it an instructional activity in literacy and language arts classes to instruct students in ways of speaking about their coursework. Examples of some types of academic language are (1) My conclusion is that _____, (2) I agree with the authors because _____, and (3) I would disagree with the _____. Mastering vocabulary and higher-order talk of a subject area requires that teachers scaffold the instruction, building on students' diverse ways of learning. This means creating a setting involving dyads and study groups, where students can practice academic language interactively.

Make time for questions. Walsh and Sattes (2005) argue that for educators to engage all students in answering questions appropriately, they must also teach new questioning behaviors to students and adopt classroom norms that support them.

Educators need to create a safe learning setting where students feel comfortable asking and answering questions. Part of the process means reminding students that all questions are important and allowing plenty of time for students to formulate, process, and answer the questions.

Through total student engagement with the teacher and peers, educators help students understand that in order to answer the big questions, they may need to address the smaller questions first. Use probing techniques to urge students to clarify their ideas and explain their reasoning. Then, challenge them with even more complex questions. Once students are accustomed to exploring and answering open-ended questions supported by evidence, take a step back and assume the role of facilitator. Teach students how to generate their own questions and encourage them to elaborate and build on each other's ideas.

Mind Games

A common command students hear is, "Remember this. . . . " Students become overwhelmed with many facts, dates, and names they need to remember. Memorizing information becomes easier when compressed in a systematic method. Some strategies that make remembering easier for students follow:

- Distribute time spent studying according to areas that need more attention.
- For classes that require memorization such as chemistry, flash cards with two names on both sides help remember two names at once.
- Using acronyms for classes such as geography makes it easier to remember. HOMES for the five lakes: Huron, Ontario, Michigan, Erie, and Superior. Other shortcuts include learning rules in English by remembering a saying such as, "Any word that fits in the blank of this sentence is a preposition: The squirrel ran _____ the tree (up, down, around, through, etc.)."

Effective Study Groups

In 2005, Valley High School in the Los Angeles County, with a Latino student enrollment of 98.1 percent, developed a successful "college-going culture" for entering ninth-grade students. The school participated in the UCLA Project, which focused on creating the conditions in urban schools needed to improve educational outcomes so that more students have access to postsecondary opportunities (McDonald & Dorr, 2006). All school personnel provide a continuous and consistent message to all students, supporting their quest for college.

McDonald and Dorr (2006) presented nine critical principles that organized the secondary schools they worked with to advance a college-going environment. Based on these principles, McDonald and Dorr developed a resource guide for creating a college-going culture, provided an action plan in the areas of college talk, information and resources, clear expectations, comprehensive counseling model, testing and curriculum, faculty involvement, family involvement, college partnerships, and articulation for building a college culture in secondary schools. The guide is a user-friendly template for schools interested in creating a college culture.

Participating in study groups is an activity that results in academic benefit. In the best of all worlds, teachers need to involve students in interactive learning activities so that students have maximum opportunity to engage and assist one another. If teachers do not have study group environments during class, they need to encourage and instruct students to form study groups.

The College Board (2011) and Cooper and Markoe-Hayes (2005) offer recommendations to facilitate effective and successful study groups among other strategies to transitions students from middle school to high school that ultimately lead to high school graduation: Students

- can clarify their notes and ask one another to fill in the missing information gaps.
- share the different talents that they bring to the group such as reading abilities, organizational skills, and capacity to memorize.
- can better solve problems together that would be very difficult to solve alone such as geometry, algebra, or physics.
- can have fun studying with others; sharing makes studying interesting. When studying is fun, students study more.

Organizing Study Groups

Some guidelines for creating and running a study group include the following:

Who: Students self-select their study groups by inviting members who share similar interests in advancing academically. These students stay alert in class, ask questions, and respond to the teacher's questions. To have an inclusive group, students should select people who understand material that is more advanced and who can explain to the group and someone who doesn't understand the material as well, who can benefit from the group's explanation. The best number for study groups seems to be four to six people. If the group is too large, not everyone gets an opportunity to participate and receive assistance.

When: Educators need to orient and supervise study groups in their setting to keep them on track. Students should meet regularly, on the same day and time each week. Being disciplined in the way they participate in the study group ensures the success of the group.

Where: Educators need to provide study groups ample space for students to meet so they can spread out their materials and be able to exchange information comfortably and adequately.

How long: Students should meet in their study groups for about two hours at a time. Having a time limit helps the group focus. Knowing that the work has to be completed within that time period helps the students focus on the task.

Educators can assist students to benefit most from study groups by helping them outline some guidelines for maximizing their group, including deciding what to accomplish at the beginning of the meetings, taking turns in leading the group, and staying focused on the tasks. In study groups, students can accomplish something that educators may not have time to provide them—consistent support to help them understand the course material.

Students receive encouragement about their peers and support their growth by coming up with different study techniques that can come in handy. In any case, peers can help encourage you to stay on track. Students often have an area that needs particular help. It can be very discouraging. In a study group, peers assist one another with that. They are there to encourage students to continue until they understand what they need to learn.

PARENT/SCHOOL/COMMUNITY PARTNERSHIPS

Giving Back to Community

Early motivation for career goals planning is an important part of preparing Latino students for college. A middle school boy in a small west Texas town near El Paso, Oscar relates his motive for becoming a doctor is to give back to his community.

When I grow up, I plan on going to a college to get a good job that pays well. But I want to be a basketball player since I'm really good at it. I really like it and that's what I'm into right now. Unless I change my mind, teaching would be my other choice because I like school. I plan on getting there by studying very hard, focusing, and listening carefully. That's what is going to be my goal until I reach it. I'll be proud of myself. I want to get lots of money. But I don't want to buy things I don't need. That is part of what I want to do to improve the world. I also want to improve the world by helping kids who are dying or need transplants or old people who need a lot of help. This is what I want to do when I grow up.

I want to become a pediatrician because helping people is one of my passions. I also like to give back to the community. I also love children. When I become a doctor, I plan on helping people in any way that I can. As a doctor I can help people who have medical needs. I believe that by helping people I will become a better person. The next reason is to give back to the community. Once I get my doctor's license, I would like to become a pediatric doctor because I like children. I like children because I believe that they are the future generation who will help me one day. By getting good grades and applying myself to school, I will soon move on to high school and college. With a high GPA and great academic standing, I will be able to attend a pre-med program in college. Afterwards, I'll enroll in medical school. I understand that the journey to medical school and as a doctor is a difficult challenge. Yet the rewarding feeling I will experience after helping those in need will be more than worth it.

He shows foresight not only for what is required in his profession but for his own needs as a senior adult. Oscar also seems cognizant of the complicated and demanding road ahead of him.

Supportive Family Member

Middle school and high school grades are difficult enough, making family support in addition to mentors even more imperative. Graciela lived in a large San Francisco–area urban city. She attended a large high school.

Mostly, I have my mother to thank for my academic success. She always found a way to help me succeed. Life has been terribly hard for my mother, my brother and me. Although, we have struggled I always remember my mom being there for us. Sometimes I would see her get home so tired that I wished I could go work also just to help her out. She always told us how important school was and used herself as an example of what happened when you did not go to college.

I was a good student, even though I was extremely shy. I would never get involved in anything and was not the type of student that would raise her hand or volunteer to do something. When I was in the middle school at Garfield, I was recommended by my teachers to participate in a summer math camp. They contacted my mom and she filled out the application and was very excited about it. At the beginning, I was kind of unsure about it because I did not know if they were going to make us stand and speak in front of the groups. They told us this program was for Latino girls who had no college role models. I found out some of my other friends had been invited to the camp so I got excited about it.

My high school had a mentor program, where I connected with a wonderful woman who was an engineer. She took me to some talks where other women in the community talked about their jobs and how they worked hard through college to get those positions. Sometimes my mother went with us and I liked that because afterwards we were able to talk with each other about the kind of career I wanted and how she felt about me wanting to be an engineer. My mentor always talked to both of us and shared how she had to find her own way through school and college because she didn't have supportive parents or someone in school to help her. This gave us a great opportunity to get close and get to know each other. I had always thought that my mother was my best friend because I was the oldest and helped her to care for my younger brothers and sisters, but working with my mentor, my mother and I got even closer. After each meeting, we went home and talked about what we heard.

I looked forward to the field trips and the picnics. We got to see places we had never seen. I really liked it when we went to visit a private catholic university and got to see a class in session. I could see myself there listening to the professor. We also went to the Union and we got to go swimming. This made me feel comfortable about the university setting. I knew that I wanted to go there because it was close to home and I didn't want to leave my mother alone with my brothers and sister. She wasn't holding me back. In fact she encouraged me to attend wherever I got accepted and could get the best education. So, if I decided to come to this university, I could really feel comfortable. The library seemed scary at first because it was so huge, but the more time I spent looking around, the more it felt like a fantasy land full of all the information I could want.

In addition, during several of our field trips, we got to talk to career people and ask them questions, such as how long it took them to get their degrees and what type of classes they had to take. It was interesting to listen to a Latino female judge, lawyer, doctor, and nurse talk to us about their lives. Some of them had lived in public housing like us! I couldn't believe it. This made me see my future plans more realistically. Sometimes I had doubts about being able to go to college because of our financial situation, but now it seemed possible. That made it more realistic for me.

Even when supportive mentors work with students like Graciela, no one can take the place of a supportive family member, especially moms. In this case, Graciela credits her mother for encouraging her to appreciate others' mentorship and help with major decisions such as college plans.

TRANSITION FROM MIDDLE TO HIGH SCHOOL

Transitioning from middle to high school requires a great deal of support for Latino students. An important activity is academic summer camps where they form strong networks with peers and find social and academic confidence.

At summer space camp: Jasmin credits her teacher and counselor for helping her get informed about special programs that will help her prepare for college and ultimately her career as an astronaut.

Since I have had a lot of love for space and stars and planets and science is my favorite subject, my life goal is to become an astronaut. I have wanted to be an astronaut since I was six years old. Space is in my heart and that is what I plan to do. My plan for getting there is to maintain my high grades and have good self-esteem. As part of my plan, I might go to 'Space Camp' this summer to learn more about space. I know I need to attend the university and not only get a bachelor's degree but a master's as well. And my parents really want me to attend a university. They say they don't want me to struggle like they do. My parents want me to have a good life with a good job. I have my goals and I'm going to work hard to reach them. To reach my goals, I have to better myself as much as I can with hard work and a good attitude. I'm not going to stop until I reach my goals. I am proud of what I can do so far because my teachers tell me that I'm a good student. I feel confident that I'm following what my heart says—shoot for the moon!

Approaching middle school, Jasmin looks forward to attending a summer Space Camp at a time when she needs reinforcement to continue not only dreaming but planning realistically for what she already anticipates will be a long preparation ahead. Clearly, she also counts on her teachers' approval as well as the encouragement from her parents.

Cooper and Markoe-Hayes (2005) report that family members, peer networks, and educators are the three prominent groups that impact students' attitudes and experiences during their transitional year into high school. They developed a scale and model that taps into a range of educational decisions that students must make while transitioning from middle to high school in order to succeed: (1) the decision to continue their education at the next level (academic predisposition); (2) the decision to engage intellectually in the coursework at the new school (academic transition); (3) the decision to pursue one's academic goals despite barriers (academic resiliency); (4) the decision to get involved in both the official and unofficial culture of the school, including extracurricular activities (social transition); and (5) the decision to abide by the rules and policies of the new school (social adjustment). Cooper and Markoe-Hayes (2005) developed a Transitional Choice Model as an attempt to develop a structure that captures the multitude of concurrent changes taking place in the academic life of adolescents during a volatile period of their lives. The model was successful in the Los Angeles–based schools. Here are two examples of other programs that support students' transition from middle to high school. The two programs include the San Jose Downtown College Prep and the Breakthrough Collaborative.

The Downtown College Prep (DCP)

Central to the theme of socializing Latino students for college is the premise that underrepresented students learn best when they are challenged academically in settings where the learning environment is organized around high expectations and an accelerated curriculum. Levin (1998) advances accelerated instruction through enrichment for all students. In the accelerated paradigm, underrepresented students are included in instructional pedagogy that is typically reserved for only the advanced or gifted students. According to Burris and Garrity (2012) and Reis, Gentry, and Maxfield (1998), academically rigorous curriculum and accelerated teaching raise the achievement even of academic under-achievers. Students perform higher than when they are taught in reme-dial programs. These foundations are the basis of the Common Core State Standards that identify higher level thinking skills in literacy, English language, science, and math as prominent in preparing students for col-lege (National Governors Association Center for Best Practices, Council of Chief State School Officers, 2010).

One example of a school that has a reputation for its accelerated pro-gram is The Downtown College Prep (DCP) in San Jose, California. It offers transition programs from middle to high school that successfully prepare Latino students for college and school. Although this is a charter school, they share comparable structures with public schools. Some of their ways of enhancing academic achievement demonstrate the educational pos-sibilities for reaching college.

A largely first-generation Latino school, DCP has two campuses. One is a charter high school and the other is a middle school (Grades 6 and 7). The mission of the schools is to ensure that all students are prepared for the rigor of college work for acceptance into four-year colleges and universities and success in college. Toward those ends, DCP is organized around specific activities that reach those goals. The rigorous learning environment includes meaningful homework, supportive atmosphere, and class size of less than 24, while the public schools typically have 30. Students sometimes enter the school unconvinced that they can keep up and achieve the college expectations. According to the principal in the middle school, those students change their minds when they understand how the DCP gives them opportunities to prove their abilities. They even like the strict expectations at DCP.

DCP students are typically those who have not yet reached their full potential—those who have had little success in a traditional school environment and who will be the first in their family to graduate from college. Educators hold a strong commitment to the philosophy of the school that every student can get to college.

Math teacher Renee Trochet describes her experience at DCP.

I teach math at DCP because I believe in its mission and its students. All students should have access to an education that helps them become numerate, logical thinkers. I earned a B.S. in Symbolic Systems at Stanford University, then spent a fifth year in the STEP Program to earn a teaching credential and M.A. in Education. Prior to my arrival at DCP, I was a web designer, tutor, and student teacher at Mission High School in San Francisco. Outside of DCP, I enjoy music, reading, going to art exhibitions, and solving puzzles of all kinds. (Downtown College Prep., 2011)

To combat the 500:1 ratio trend of Latinos going to college, DCP educators feel strongly about the opportunities they offer. They provide lots of hand holding, which translates to significant support. Students have to design a plan and commitment to go to college and their plan of action that will get through school.

An inspiring story from one of DCP's graduates comes from Pauline Fernandez, Class of 2008. Her mother enrolled her in DCP in the tenth grade with the desire she get a college degree. Pauline's mother was diagnosed with a brain tumor and died when Pauline was a senior. Following her mother's death, Pauline lived with neighbors. She graduated and attended a local community college, by taking two jobs to support herself. She plans to transfer to San Jose State University. Pauline uses her mother's dream of a college education to motivate herself. Pauline's desire is to learn—not just earn credits. In fact, she asked one math teacher to fail her so she could take the class again to get a better grasp of the concepts (Downtown College Prep., 2008). Pauline had the same rigorous curriculum through high school as her peers.

DCP academic activities assist students in learning to read, collect, and analyze information independently. They acquire strategies to think systematically about the information. Their verbal skills to articulate their thinking also improve. And very importantly, students achieve proficiency on standards-based English Language Arts Content courses.

DCP students learn to adopt the schools values of *ganas* (desire), *comunidad* (community), and *orgullo* (pride). These values are familiar and congruent between the school and home. *Ganas* inspires students to work to the best of their ability. *Comunidad* gives them a purpose to work toward and recognize that they have a place where they belong. It has a shared history, language, and ideals. *Orgullo* focuses students on their sense of self-respect, which propels them forward with confidence.

Breakthrough Collaborative

Since 1978, the Breakthrough Collaborative (BC) is a national non-profit group that has changed the lives of more than 20,000 students in 33 locations across the country. Sixty-eight percent of the students qualify for free or reduced school lunch. The Collaborative accepts high-potential, low-income students who are the first in their family to attend college. Ninety-two percent of the BC students are students of color. Thirty-four percent speak English as a second language. And thirty-nine percent live in single-parent households. BC communicates with middle and high schools where BC students attend since they track students' academic performance and needs.

The Collaborative has two main program groups—middle school students and the high school or college-aged teachers who instruct and mentor them. Students apply for admission in the summer of their seventh-grade year and continue until they graduate from high school, when students are making key decisions about college. In the middle school, the Collaborative helps middle school students thrive in the top college preparatory high schools in their communities. They attend two 6-week, academically intense summer sessions, year-round tutoring, and continuous college preparation and assistance.

Summer sessions have a class size of 3:1 in subjects, including English literature, math, science, social studies, and foreign language. They receive at least two hours of nightly homework, attend field trips on Friday, and attend family outreach events.

Throughout the school year, students receive after-school academic tutoring and skill building in math and writing along with mentoring. Once they enter high school, students have ongoing college prep assistance for them and their parents. Some of the workshop topics include financial aid, scholarship opportunities, and admissions counseling.

BC identifies three major factors that portend students' success factors in middle school through high school, on their way to college: (1) the belief in the need for college, (2) peer group influences, and (3) the rigor of high school coursework. The Collaborative addresses ways to ensure that the students who apply are truly serious about a four-year college future. It pays recruitment visits to students' homes, stressing the need for college. Students undergo a rigorous application process, including interviews and reference checks. This also includes the staff talking with students and families about college aspirations. Since students are four times more likely to enroll in college if a majority of their friends also plan to attend, the mentoring and tutoring is done by high school and college-aged students to create a strong peer-oriented learning environment (FINE Webinar, 2011). Additionally, the focus on an academically challenging curriculum involves not only mentoring and tutoring but also a summer program for six weeks. The Breakthrough staff also helps students and families understand and plan high school courses to meet college prerequisites.

Students commit to maintain a "B" average through school. They need to commit to the Collaborative goals of attending a four-year college or university. Students submit transcripts for review twice a year. Students are required to contact the BC staff when they're struggling in classes or if they receive grades of "C" or below.

Teacher Veronica Alvarez gives insights about her experience as a teacher in the summer programs.

I have chosen to work in places with objectives similar to Breakthrough's. My own aspirations were shaped by my experiences at the Collaborative, where students' talents, equality, and commitment are truly valued. I attribute my first summer at Breakthrough to my interest in going into urban education. The kids were smart and funny, and their parents were amazing. High Tech High is project-based learning. It is a total team effort, and everyone is committed to the same end.

For two 6-week periods in the summer, students receive intense instruction from committed teachers such as Veronica Alvarez, who believe that all students have the ability to get to college, if they get the necessary support (Breakthrough Collaborative, 2012).

Santa Fe, New Mexico, is one of the Collaborative's 27 sites. The Santa Fe Preparatory students begin in a summer program in sixth and seventh grades. They take English, science, math, and history. Some electives include Model Rocketry, the Chemistry of Food, Green Slime (a class about biology and keeping amphibious creatures as pets), poetry, and game theory. The program challenges students to achieve more than they thought possible.

"Before Breakthrough, I saw myself as a student that could just do enough work to get by, but now I can push myself further than ever."

—Diana, eighth grade

"Breakthrough made me appreciate education and school, it made me think about my education and my future."

—Annai, ninth grade

During the regular school year, BC Santa Fe continues its support by holding weekly after-school tutoring sessions. Once in high school, students have the option of signing up for college prep courses and attending workshops that focus on college preparation. They receive the support and guidance they need to realize their dream of going to college.

The committed teachers are exceptional high school and college students. They know it what takes to make it. Sonal, a teacher, taught in the summer program in 2004 and 2006. She recounts,

When a student who was told she was too stupid to learn math becomes your highest performing student of the summer—when you see a shy student taking charge of a group activity in your classroom—when the third lesson plan you developed to teach a tricky topic finally succeeds—when on the last day the kids and teachers leave with tears in their eyes—it is moments like this that make Breakthrough an important experience for its teachers. (Breakthrough Santa Fe, 2012)

Students can participate in a full year of activities. While the summer experience allows the students to work at an accelerated pace away from their traditional classroom setting, once they return to their regular setting, they continue to receive support and guidance through academic tutoring, parent participation workshops, and mentoring toward their goal of college admission.

REFLECTIONS

Preparing middle and high school students can take many directions. However, to ensure that students arrive to college, several conditions have shown to be most effective in the process. Regardless of how the program is organized, the necessary features are tutoring, mentoring, and offering advanced courses; students should also develop good study habits and skills as well as parent/school partnerships. One of the most significant elements in an organized effort is providing a supportive academic transition from middle through high school. The examples in this chapter illustrate that all programs support and supplement the public school efforts. They are adjunct endeavors that serve Latino students to reach college. The values and expectations that drive the educational strategies in the programs described are not foreign to public schools and offer important lessons for public school educators in organizing programs to strengthen the potential of students who need extra encouragement as well as additional and continuous support to reach their goal.

BEST PRACTICES FOR EDUCATORS

Rigorous High School Coursework

- According to the Breakthrough Collaborative, rigorous high school coursework accounts for the greatest impact on a bachelor's degree completion.
- Educators need to work jointly with parents to inform them about the proper course sequencing and ensuring that students take the necessary prerequisite courses at the correct time.

Key Lessons for Educators

- Help students and parents raise their expectations for achievement.
- Inform students and families on the importance of college, their required coursework, college affordability, and resources for obtaining financial aid.
- Teach parents to recognize and demand high-quality education.
- Teach parents to be advocates for their children.

Inquiry in the Classroom

Practical questioning strategies involve interactive approaches not only between the teacher and student but also between students (Classroom Questioning, 2011).

Clarifying the lesson: Students can ask questions on material that is unclear. Pass out three-by-five cards to the students and ask them to write down anything in a lesson that is unclear or confusing. Collect the cards at the end of the lecture and provide feedback (and elaboration) during the next class meeting.

Asking random students: Write all the students' names on three-by-five cards. Then, shuffle the cards. As you go through the lesson, select a card from the stack for each question.

Peers asking questions: Students learn from asking each other questions. Ask students to write their answers to a complex question on a piece of paper. Then, ask the students to confer with their neighbor to defend their answers.

Coursework in a College Culture

The Downtown College Prep typical course sequencing includes the following schedule. There are a variety of options at each level, depending on the individual student's skills.

Ninth Grade

- All students take English I, Algebra I, and College Readiness.
- Students who test below a sixth-grade reading level take Verbal Reasoning; the rest take Spanish or Journalism.
- Students who test below a seventh-grade math level take Numeracy I; the rest take Integrated Science.

Tenth Grade

- All students take English II, World History, and a visual/performing arts class (Dance, Photography, or Studio Art).
- Students who test below an eighth grade reading level take Verbal Reasoning II; the rest take the appropriate level of Spanish.
- Students who have passed Algebra I take Algebra II (or Algebra II Accelerated) and Biology (as Algebra I is a prerequisite for Biology). The rest repeat Algebra I and take Numeracy II or Journalism (if their numeracy skills are at grade level).

Eleventh Grade

- All students take English III (or English III Honors) and U.S. History. Students continue to take Spanish (this is optional if they have met the two-year requirement).
- Students who passed Algebra I as tenth graders now take Algebra II. Those who passed Algebra II as tenth graders take Geometry. Some students choose to accelerate and take Geometry during the summer after tenth grade and now take Precalculus.
- Students who have passed Biology take Chemistry; the rest take Biology. Students take additional electives, depending on where they are in meeting their requirements.

Twelfth Grade

- All students take English IV (or AP English Language).
- Students who have not yet taken Geometry do so now. The rest choose between Precalculus, College Prep Math, or Calculus.
- Students take additional electives, depending on where they are in meeting their requirements. Senior-level electives available include American Government, AP U.S. History, Latin American Studies, Biology, Journalism, any visual/performing arts class, any Spanish class.

Features
and Activities of
Successful Programs

6

Effective college culture stresses college knowledge—the information, inspiration, and preparation that shapes students' understanding of concepts of college as a vehicle. Many Latino students get to middle and high school grades without any knowledge about what college means. Whether formally or informally organized, educators and parents are students' key supporters as Sarita shares about her relationship with her parents and high school counselor in addition to the mentor role they played in getting her to make college plans.

I don't recall ever hearing the word *college* in my family or in school. My parents went to school in Mexico but only to the sixth grade. When they came to the United States, they expected their children to do well in school. I think my parents encouraging me helped me because I when I got into high school a counselor called me into her office. She told me that I had very good grades in all of my classes especially in my advanced math and science courses. Then she asked me what my college plans were. I told her that I didn't have any because my parents couldn't afford it. She said that I should decide what I wanted to do in my career. I tried to talk to my parents about my plans for college when I was a junior in high school, but after many attempts, I finally asked my mom why she avoided me. She answered in Spanish, 'Nosotros no podemos discutir eso del colegio porque nosotros no sabemos y tenemos miedo decirte algo mal' (We can't discuss college with you because we don't know about that and we're afraid to tell you something wrong). I told Mom that I wanted to go to college and that my counselor said that I should make plans. My mom said that they couldn't afford it, but if I could find a way to do it, that I had their blessing. I got so excited and so was my counselor when I told her. She helped me with lots of information about careers and colleges and how to apply for scholarships. She also gave me the name of a group in our high school where students got together to talk about college admission with the counselors.

An interested counselor and supportive parents encouraged Sarita to take steps toward getting informed and involved in the college planning and application process. Her counselor was supportive and recognized Sarita's potential. For the many Saritas whose parents cannot instruct them and the many counselors who sometimes have to play the sole role in guiding students, guidelines exist on how programs can organize to best instruct and direct students toward college.

GUIDELINES FOR SUCCESSFUL
ACADEMIC PROGRAMS FOR LATINOS

In 1999, First Lady Hillary Clinton convened a group of Latino educators at the White House Initiative on Educational Excellence for Hispanic Americans (United States Department of Education, 1999). The participants identified the salient characteristics of successful programs that serve Latino youth have in common. A brief summary of six of its features follows.

1. Appoint dedicated professional Latino leaders and define program outcomes.

Programs must have well-trained professional staff to design and manage the program. This includes establishing short-, medium-, and long-term goals to measure progress, confront obstacles, and implement policies to achieve their purpose. The importance of Latino staff is that people from a similar background can offer an understanding about the dynamics of the home, school, and community for Latino youth. This enables them to attain their program goals. The leadership team needs to be familiar with the best available professional practices in the field. Informed staff that seeks to stay current about best practices are more effective in designing and adapting interventions that make a lasting difference.

2. Utilize Spanish language and local culture in program activities.

The bicultural and bilingual component in most of the programs helps adults and children communicate better and become familiar with their language, culture, and heritage. Providing services in the native language to students and families fosters an appreciation for other cultures, builds self-esteem, and includes parents in the service delivery and youth development process.

Integrating Latino culture and cultural awareness into services and programs helps Latino youth navigate differences between the culture of the home, the community, and the school. This helps Latino youth deal with the challenges posed by peer pressure and the experience of racism, while imparting a positive view of their own culture, respect for others, and a positive educational experience.

3. Engage parents, family, and community resources.

Successful programs make an effort to understand family circumstances and establish communication with parents. Parental education and involvement gives the parents an understanding of the cumulative nature of the child development process and gives them information about program design, management, and goals (Delgado Gaitan, 2004). A sense of inclusion and ownership of the programs also empowers parents with the tools they need to become better caregivers and assist their children beginning in the early years and continuing up the grades. Empowerment occurs when Latino parents have a place in the educational decisions that need to be made on behalf of their children. That said, empowerment is not a commodity that one group gives to another. It is a consciousness that parents arrive at and exercise to accomplish what they need to improve their children's education. They do not blindly accept the school's definition of their role. Ways in which parents empower themselves is to organize themselves apart from the school's definition of "parent involvement group." They set their own agendas separate from those that schools design and negotiate their role with the school. That is, in most parent engagement models, schools still define the parents' role in their children's education. However, parents can determine their specific function in the social context. Effective parent involvement programs empowering Latino families promote high aspirations for students and strong commitment to lifelong learning, as well as discipline in their schoolwork.

Parent education programs help parents become more involved in the education of their children by providing information about the various elements of child development, access to and information on the public school system, parenting tools and skills, and English language instruction by increasing awareness of the social services and community resources available to them. These practices have been effective in creating accelerated learning environments leading to healthy child development, which boosts parental efficacy and self-esteem and engages parents in their children's educational development. Such programs produce better academic outcomes as a result from the increased parental involvement.

Successful programs for Latino youth have moved away from cultural deficit models and now recognize the talent, strength, creativity, and resiliency of Latino families and youth. School-based programs acknowledge the talent of Latinos. They establish strong networks with other stakeholders, including other local schools and colleges, health care clinics, nonprofit programs, and organizations.

According to the participants at the Initiative on Educational Excellence for Hispanic Americans, youth do better if they know that at least one other adult has a strong stake and interest in their personal, educational, and long-term success. Students respond because they realize that someone cares and that someone likes them. They are able to get help, guidance, encouragement, and support when they need it.

Many programs provide youth with opportunities to make a contribution and participate in the design of civic and community activities. Youth perform best under clear rules and expectations, when they feel central to the program, when they have a stake in the design, development, and implementation of the rules, and when they receive acknowledgment for their contributions and clear rewards.

4. Assess and evaluate programs systematically.

Successful organizations use research to help in the design, management, and evaluation of their programs and initiatives. This involvement allows the organization to systematically examine their programs, learn from their experience, understand better the needs of participating youth and other stakeholders, and design effective programs.

5. Documenting and publicizing

Successful programs and organizations have the ability to document and publicize their organization, services, programs, and positive results. The programs reviewed in this publication demonstrate that the number and visibility of professionals, groups, organizations, and service providers making a difference in the Latino community have increased appreciably in recent years. There are many community-based organizations with significant experience in the design, development, management, and evaluation of programs that help build, maintain, and rejuvenate Latino communities and that make a difference for Latino youth. These programs are assets to the nation and it is important to draw on their knowledge, experience, and resources to build leadership around Latino child and youth development issues.

   6. Disseminating results

   Last but not least, a feature defining successful academic programs for Latino youth is the process of obtaining and designating adequate funding for the program. Having sufficient organizational resources is essential to effective services for Latino youth.
   Every successful educational program is based on the effectiveness of the various components of the program design, including academic counseling, parent education, application and financial assistance workshops, and career planning (Gandara & Biel, 2001). The programs discussed in this chapter focus on the type of activities that the various programs implement. This includes successful structures and strategies as well as lessons that public schools can garner.

EFFECTIVE PROGRAMS

Numerous educational programs have a strong reputation for succeeding in preparing students for college. Three such programs are Advancement Via Individual Determination (AVID), Upward Bound, and the East Bay Consortium (EBC). They represent three categories of programs—national large, midsize and expanding, and small regional. They all share some common guiding principles, delineated and advanced by a group of invited educational experts at a White House meeting on Educational Excellence for Hispanic Americans in 1999. Public schools can glean important lessons from these projects to incorporate in their school curriculum such as mentor programs, parent involvement, and tutorials.

ADVANCEMENT VIA INDIVIDUAL DETERMINATION (AVID)

The Advancement Via Individual Determination (AVID) Director of Professional Development, Dr. Aliber Lozano, shares his personal story of growing up in a family and community with educational challenges and important support systems that helped him excel. Dr. Lozano's father immigrated to the United States at the age of 28 and had a third-grade education. He married his mother, who had dropped out of the eighth grade. About learning from his parents and family, Dr. Lozano says:

> I believe my parents to be among the most educated people I know. Their lessons did not come from text books, but from life, working as migrant farmworkers, raising five children and helping support and guide my father's mother and eight brothers and sisters who eventually came to the United States as well.

Dr. Lozano's father had wise words about education for his children, "Lo único que les puedo dejar es una educación (The one thing I could leave you is an education)." His words echoed in his children throughout their educational journey. Dr. Lozano recalls,

> Though he rarely spoke to us, he repeated these words to us, often at the end of the day after working in the fields. The first time I heard these words was as my mother and I walked out the car and toward Sacred Heart, my first day of preschool.
>
> I enjoyed school and overall had a very positive experience throughout my primary and secondary education. Toward the end of the school year, I would have to check out of school and check into another school that was near the area to which my family had migrated. By my own constructed definition, I was a good student. I came to this conclusion because I knew my older sister was a good student, receiving academic recognition at school and home. [She] would not only guide my academic success in public school but would later navigate my entry into college.
>
> Out of five children in our family, three of us have a college degree. My youngest brother, Aaron, has a bachelor's degree and is a high school journalism and speech and communication teacher. My only sister has two master's degrees and is an assistant principal at a high school. Both my oldest sister and youngest brother work on AVID campuses.
>
> My charge is to defy the odds and close the achievement and opportunity gaps, as I have experienced firsthand with my family and friends. One doctorate out of ten students should not be the exception, 100 percent should be the expectation, no matter what the ethnic background, socioeconomic status, or other variables, we as educators cannot change. What we can change is their social and academic preparation and our expectations. (Lozano, 2008, pp. 2–3)

As an AVID administrator, Dr. Lozano is the living testament to the possibilities that the program offers. Since its inception in 1980, AVID has served more than 400,000 in elementary, middle, and high schools across this country and even sixteen other countries. Although it is designed to serve all students, it focuses on the least served students in middle and high school.

In 1980, Mary Catherine Swanson, an English teacher in San Diego acted on her conviction to bring 32 inner-city students to her class at Clairemont High School to prepare them academically. Mrs. Swanson's curriculum, based on "best practices" incorporates strategies that underserved students' need.

There began AVID's primary mission—to serve the historically underserved students. They receive literacy using the Writing, Inquiry, Collaboration, Reading (WICR) program. The principles teach students: (1) writing to learn, (2) inquiry to learn, and (3) reading to learn. These strategies become central to the daily instructional practices. For example, in a subject such as writing, students are not just taught to write, they are taught to use writing as a strategy to learn. Academic components also emphasize the brainstorming of possibilities for students to imagine their future. Increasing students' level of confidence in academic environments empowers them to make intelligent choices in their academic planning.

AVID's philosophy is based on research methods, a delivery system that is coherent, consistent, collaborative, and assessable. A seminal part of AVID is high expectations. Teachers expect students to perform academic skills at high levels, thus improving the quality of their work. Consistently using these strategies supports students to internalize the skills and be able to adapt to more challenging learning situations. AVID also assists educators to implement, monitor, and measure pedagogical practices used to prepare students for college. Continuous assessment allows teachers to determine the effectiveness of their instruction.

With respect to Latino students across the 48 states, AVID reports that 89 percent of Latino students that have been a part of the program in at least two years of high school plan to attend college compared to 22 percent of counterparts that do not attend AVID (AVID, 2012).

Districts Commit to AVID Principles

AVID expects school districts to implement specific strategies. At the 2009 JUNTOS Conference, AVID explained what school districts need in order to collaborate with the Program (Roberts, 2009). AVID requires them to follow an educational philosophy, including collaboration, real-life application, bilingualism, and valuing cultural diversity in elementary, middle, and high school.

Elementary school level components: Along with the WICR curriculum, elementary schools prepare students in basic academic skills and partnerships. Educators hold high expectations for underserved students. This includes encouraging students to learn to make predictions about their future. Elementary schools expose students to museums and college campuses to stimulate their curiosity to connect their experience to their studies.

Students are expected to successfully develop expertise in communication, educational self-advocacy, and study skills. Organizational skills include mental, organizational tools such as time management, goal setting, and note taking. The steps needed to make AVID successful include teachers reaching out to families and to other grade-level teachers to coordinate curriculum.

Elementary school site administrators are required to participate in a two-year training cycle with AVID District Leadership Training. Some elementary school districts feed into middle and secondary sites that partner with AVID.

Middle school components: Like elementary schools, middle AVID schools require educators to encourage students to take the time to enjoy middle school and not be in a rush to grow up, while preparing them to map their choices for future success in school. These activities help students reduce their discomfort in the middle school. When students feel emotionally secure, they concentrate on learning.

AVID focuses intently on middle schools because 70 percent of AVID middle school students are Latino or African American. In Pleasant Valley Middle School in Wichita, Kansas, the English for Speakers of Other Languages (ESOL) student population comprises 34 percent. The school provides these students with the opportunity to participate in high rigor, including advanced placement language arts, honors math, and pre-algebra, that advanced classes offer. At Pleasant Valley, educators believe that the WICR strategies provide the academic rigor students need. They utilize them schoolwide to challenge and engage every student. Teachers sometimes modify WICR instructional strategies to meet students' learning modalities, thus supporting them to progressively increase their levels of learning.

One success story from Pleasant Valley Middle School is Ismael. Staff reports,

> He is a newcomer student from El Salvador who arrived at Wichita in 2010. In less than two years after his arrival he was among the 35 percent of the English as a Second Language (ESL) population chosen to be in our AVID program. Ismael excelled in rigorous courses and has assumed strong leadership roles in

AVID. He was accepted into AVID and placed in Pre-AP Language Arts. He has flourished in all areas with a 4.0 grade point average. (AVID, 2011)

High school components: In committing to work with AVID, high schools agree to provide a budget for training, materials, and activities to ensure quality application of all AVID components. In this high school level, teachers work with students as they get closer to graduating and making decisions about college. They help reduce or eliminate students' fear of leaving the familiarity of the high school classroom and the security of families if they choose to go away to college. The AVID program believes that students will make a smooth transition to the college setting by following a rigorous curriculum and becoming as informed as possible about college life. And in the high school years, they are surrounded by a support system in and out of school, saturating them with the necessary academic scaffolding as the Mount Vernon High School example illustrates.

When demographics changed in Mount Vernon High in Mount Vernon, Washington, creating a school culture became necessary. Demographic changes mandated the increase of AP courses from 1 AP course in 2003 to 11 in 2010. The most encouraging statistic is that the enrollment of Latino students in AP courses increased from 0 in 2003 to more than 170 students in 2010. Through AVID, Mount Vernon educators committed to increasing student engagement to help students and staff establish mentoring relationships. Through this process, educators, advisors, and parents develop "a high school and beyond plan." Both parents and students become knowledgeable about the pathway needed to attend a four-year college and take appropriate steps in that direction.

In sum, AVID supports students to accelerate their learning. AVID's use of research-based methods of effective instruction provides professional development and promotes systemic reform and change in school districts. Not only does AVID collaborate with school districts to improve the academic standing and college possibilities for underprepared students, but it also advocates to states and federal legislatures to fund research on programs like AVID to ensure the success of Latinos and all student groups with special needs. As of the 2009–2010 school year, AVID is implemented in more than 898 school districts across the United States as well as in various other countries.

UPWARD BOUND

As part of the War on Poverty campaign, Upward Bound emerged in response to a nation which demanded solutions to the educational needs of the chronically poor students. Upward Bound's goal is to increase the rate at which participants complete high school and enroll in college. It serves all high school students that meet the criteria. Students come from families with low income and where neither parent holds a bachelor's degree. The program prepares students to succeed in their precollege academic performance and ultimately in their college pursuits.

Students attend computer classes and career curriculum clusters. Before graduating from high school, juniors and seniors visit and tour up to six colleges and universities. Key Upward Bound classes include mathematics, laboratory sciences, composition, literature, and foreign languages. Other academic support activities such as tutoring, counseling, mentoring, cultural enrichment, work-study programs, financial and economic literacy empower students to feel confident during the college application process. Additionally, Upward Bound focuses on students who are limited English proficient, students with disabilities, students who are homeless, in foster care or aging out of the foster care system, as well as other disenfranchised students. The San Antonio example illustrates the connections between students, community, and Upward Bound.

San Antonio, Texas, Upward Bound

Admission to Upward Bound, San Antonio, requires that students complete the eighth grade, be between the ages of 13 and 19 (except veterans), and have a need for academic support in order to pursue a program of postsecondary education. Students are selected based on recommendations from local educators, social workers, clergy, or other interested parties. The San Antonio program is comprised of three parts: math and science, academic year, and summer program. Throughout the academic year, a counselor advises program participants and provides necessary preparation for college entry. Students also attend college tours and cultural events to further expand their awareness about college.

During the school year, students attend weekly tutorials. Any Upward Bound student receiving below a "C" grade in any college preparatory class must attend tutoring for one hour each week for each class below a "C" grade. If students find themselves needing tutoring, they need only request it. Procedures for Upward Bound tutoring require students to submit their request to the Upward Bound tutoring office at the university. Students also indicate the day and time that they can come attend their tutoring session.

The academic support component of Upward Bound, San Antonio, is designed to enrich the students' academic skills with a concentration in math and science courses. Students are also exposed to computer technology, English, and foreign languages as part of the program curriculum. Statistics show that the program has an average annual high school graduation rate of 98 percent. Over 90 percent attend college, and many receive scholarships and financial aid.

EAST BAY CONSORTIUM

The East Bay Consortium (EBC) of Educational Institutions, Inc. is one of 15 California Student Opportunity and Access Projects (Cal-SOAP) administered by the California Student Aid Commission. Eight middle and high schools in the greater Oakland area participate in the tutoring component of the EBC. The EBC serves students of all ethnic groups if they are from families with low incomes or families with a history of low college attendance rates. One of the biggest academic challenges that EBC addresses in serving over 9,000 students is the transition of students from middle school to high school, noting that about 60 percent of middle school students who have a 2.5 GPA or higher in the middle school drop below 2.5 if they enter high school without the academic support necessary to compete in high school classes. Mentors and tutors are indispensable for this group. In spite of the challenging students that EBC serves, it reports an 84 percent success rate of students who participate in the program entering college (Montenegro, 2011).

Tutors go into classrooms to work closely with teachers in assisting all students who sign up to impact on the student's achievement. After-school tutoring is also available at each site; the school advertises the service and all students are highly encouraged to participate. Students can get help in any subject, including English, math, science, and social studies. College students mentor an average of eight students. They follow up on the student's academic progress in school and engage them in activities that encourage them to continue to do well in school. Other EBC activities include college field trips, completing college and financial aid applications, participating in leadership conferences, and attending social activities. Not only are students prepared for college, but EBC also recognizes that teachers are a critical piece of the college-bound culture. It empowers teachers to teach in inventive ways. In total, EBC encompasses several components available to all students and teachers.

EBC Student Programs

The East Bay Consortium offers a variety of programs both in and out of school.

Tutoring—EBC provides after-school tutoring as well as in-class tutoring to students at the eight participating middle and high schools in Oakland.

Mentoring—A Saturday morning mentorship program assists students with guidance and to make decisions about their life choices.

Saturday Program—The Pre-Collegiate Academy (PCA) has weekly sessions for students and their families to engage in hands-on learning activities.

College Advising—EBC provides high school and college advising to students through college centers located at two high schools and through workshops presented at schools upon request.

Counselor Community Connection Live (CCC Live)—EBC sponsors a live cable television show on Oakland Unified School District's KDOL Channel 27.

Family Math and Science—On a weekly basis, students and parents are involved in hands-on math and science. Throughout the year, the EBC holds informational workshops open to all interested parents. These workshops provide information about what students can do as early as middle school to prepare for college, how parents can support their college-bound student, financial aid and scholarships that will help fund their child's education, and more.

Pre-Collegiate Academy (PCA)—A comprehensive program working with students, teachers, prospective teachers, and parents through middle school and high school to increase their academic skills and prepare them for admission into higher education institutions.

Transfer: Making It Happen (TMIH)—A program designed to inform high school and community college students about the opportunities and process of transferring to a four-year college or university from a community college.

I'm Going To College (IGTC)—This program involves upper grade elementary school students to provide them basic information about college as well as a hands-on college experience. An example is 160 students from Jefferson Elementary School in the Oakland School District that took a field trip to the University of California, Berkeley (UCB). Participants share about their experience (East Bay Consortium, 2011).

The fifth-grade students were prepared on what college is, what a major is, and what financial aid is available. Teacher, Mr. Davis explains, "Most of them have no idea what college is about. Some of them are a little afraid. . . . "

Another teacher, Adelita, commented, "They have to think ahead because you have to save for it. Other students they're competing against are from a different environment."

Prior to the field trip, student Gina describes how she imagines that UC Berkeley will be like, "I think it's a big school with a big yard."

Teacher A. Martinez speaks about the importance of these field trips, "You start thinking about it [college] early. They have to compete with kids from very different places and backgrounds."

Once on campus, Ms. Larkirith, from the Undergraduate Admissions Office greeted the students. She emphasized, "I'm Going to College (IGTC) is a very strong statement. And you can continue in that state of mind on what you're going to do after you get out of high school. It's something that's more than saying, 'I want to go to college.' It's a given, you're all going to go to college. And I hope you all come here."

During their visit, Noerena, a sociology student, spoke to the students, sharing with them a glimpse what to look for in their future. "Imagine yourself going down this hallway and at the end are many doors. And if you have a college education, you can open any door."

One parent, Mrs. Moran, who accompanied the IGTC group on their field trip, felt very encouraged by the prospect of her child attending college. "I came today because it's important for me to gear my son to go to college. It's a good opportunity for him. I think it's important for them to do something with their lives. I wasn't able to go, so I want him to go."

Students walked around campus with their IGTC backpacks filled with school supplies. They sat in classes taught by volunteers, ate pizza at lunch, and played ball. After a full day, a student gave his impression about college, "You get to pick your classes and they have lots of classes you can take."

REFLECTIONS

Building college-bound curriculums in schools needs to be a definitive goal. Students share how programs such as Advancement Via Individual Determination, Upward Bound, and the East Bay Consortium open the window to the importance and success of college programs that extend the high school curriculum and support system. Through students' participation in these programs, their decision and commitment to go to college is not left up to chance. The effectiveness of programs discussed here rests on the strength of structural programmatic features such as employing well-prepared personnel, engaging parents, utilizing students' language and culture, as well as conducting ongoing assessment and evaluation. These programs serve many public school students and educators. Thus, it is important that the links between the programs and schools endure. Above all, students feel that personnel in these programs believe in them and support them with the resources they need to stretch out and reach their goal—admission to college.

BEST PRACTICES FOR CREATING COLLEGE CULTURE IN SCHOOLS

AVID Barriers and Practical Best Practices (Martinez, 2008, pp. 8–9)

AVID has developed an understanding of several schoolwide issues in teaching ELL Latino students and best practices to address them.

Issue: Counselors overburdened with caseloads

Resolve: Identify and train bilingual staff members to serve as counselors to ELL students, including monitoring their progress, supporting them, and collaborating with teachers of Latino students.

Issue: Misinterpretation of foreign students with transcripts

Resolve: Many students often have to repeat courses because school personnel do not give them proper course credit. Thus, schools can provide training of counselors and registrars so that they can better support new student arrivals from Mexico or other Spanish-speaking countries. This practice can extend districtwide.

Issue: Long-term ELL status

Resolve: ELL students often remain in remedial ELL classes. ELL teachers need training on AVID ELL curriculum and how to guide students to achieve English proficiency and successfully get into accelerated all-English classes.

Issue: Lack of time for college-bound immigrant students

Resolve: The goal should be for Latino students to extend beyond high school. Develop a high school plan for each student that places Latino ELL students in classes that follow the rigorous

AVID curriculum. Ensure that the plan helps students meet college entrance requirements.

Issue: Lack of involvement in school

Resolve: Follow the AVID model for the Spanish-speakers' classes, creating a nurturing, supportive environment. Make ELL students part of planning school activities that they can participate in, to integrate students on campus.

Issue: Parents unfamiliar with U.S. educational system

Resolve: Personally invite parents to school and provide them with the information and resources needed to support their child's effort to obtain a college degree. Make the workshops culturally relevant, arranging for Spanish-speaking guides who can address parent concerns and alleviate their fears.

SUGGESTIONS FOR ELEMENTARY AND SECONDARY EDUCATORS

Educators can facilitate contact with organizations such as Upward Bound and East Bay Consortia:

- Inform high school Latino students about local organizations that provide academic, emotional, and financial support toward college.
- Hold informational workshops for Latino parents on how to find organizational resources to assist their young people in their college pursuits.

Collaborations
and Partnerships

7

After graduating from Hidalgo Early College High School, Hector heads for University of Texas–Pan American with 72 college credits to his name and the University's Presidential Scholarship in hand. His major will be in mechanical engineering. Hector's history teachers have told him that he has such talent for history that he should major in it in college. His science teachers have encouraged him to do the same in sciences. And his love for math and calculus has led him to engineering. He believes that mechanical engineering somehow combines all his passions. By all accounts, Hector is an academically outstanding student with great promise. However, his personal home life has been less than ideal. Hector's stepfather and mother died within a year of each other when he was about ten years old. He was orphaned with two younger sisters. Fortunately, his grandmother moved in to care for the three children.

Hector's passion for learning is demonstrated in his appetite for reading not only books related to his mechanical engineering major and career pursuits but also his love of science, math, and history. He explains,

> I don't have money to buy new books, but there is a dump near our neighborhood and people who move away dump lots of good stuff there and I pick up all the books I can get like books on history and adventure like Jules Verne's books. They're in good shape so I'm happy to take them. I also get good deals online for used books.

Getting a computer was also a learning experience for Hector and his friends. *"There are plenty of computers you can buy in the flea market for about $100. So my friends and I went and got our computers there and we learned how to repair them and get them in top working order."* Using these same creative and intelligent skills, Hector and his friends help each other to maintain their cars. *"I need to keep up my car since it's got to get me to college,*

35 miles away. I can't move out right now because my sisters are still in high school and they need lot of support."

Hector is grateful to educators at Hidalgo Early College High School for their support. *"They helped me to figure out what to do when I shared with them my doubts about what would happen to me and my sisters. They were so understanding and showed me how I could work out things in my life so I could go to college and get a good career."* After all, Hector remains hopeful that his hard work and love of learning will steer him toward his goals, to get his career and help his sisters also do the same.

With the exception of the parents' death, Hector's story mirrors that of many students and their families who live in that area. Hidalgo and surrounding towns comprise an agricultural community, where substandard housing serves as home for children who attend Hidalgo schools. Often, parents cannot afford paper and pencils, much less computers (Nodine, 2010). So how have these families supported educators to set their expectations, not on their children's high school graduation but on college graduation and a professional career?

Families have passed bonds to support the district's facilities that have made schools a welcoming place for children. As they walk around their schools, the message about planning for college is strong. On their way to the cafeteria, students see banners lining the hallways. They read, "College and Career Readiness: Our Future Begins Today." Banners from many universities remind students about their choices for colleges—UT Austin, Texas A&M, Harvard, Stanford, Notre Dame, Michigan, and many others.

Educators instruct parents on how to create a study place for their children at home. Equally important, both parents and educators agree on ways to help students shape a college-focused vision and attitude by instilling in them the idea their power resides within them. One example is that teachers tell their students "You're a doctor. Realize yourself." This puts college into students' thinking every day along with pens and notebooks that students receive from colleges and universities when they write to those institutions to request information.

Schools alone could not possibly provide students all the resources necessary to prepare them for college. However, through sustained partnerships between schools and organized local, state, or national programs, Latino students can better obtain the necessary resources to guide them along the road to college. The partnerships described in this chapter are success stories that speak to program planners at all levels—superintendents, coordinators, teachers, counselors, board members, college administrators, as well as parents—because the efforts described here involve the combined efforts of these many professionals. Hidalgo Independent Schools (HIS), Puente, and GEAR UP represent distinct sizes and models of operation. That is, Hidalgo is a local school district program, Puente is a statewide effort, and GEAR UP has over 200 partnerships across the country. Although they vary in their structural organization and the resources they provide, they also share some common effective strategies that I've discussed in previous chapters. Readers can appreciate how these programs and the lessons they take away may relate to respective settings.

HIDALGO INDEPENDENT SCHOOLS: A SCHOOL DISTRICT SUCCESS STORY

Hidalgo is a well-recognized and highly praised program that takes different approaches to achieving their goal, graduating underrepresented students from college. Hidalgo ISD once ranked among the worst performing districts in the state, but now it is one of the most successful (Hamilton, 2010). This is due in part to an exceptional level of collaboration between local leaders in public and higher education.

In south Texas, the Hidalgo Independent School District (ISD) has raised the bar on what it means for a public school system to focus on college readiness. Hidalgo ISD is comprised of four elementary, one middle, and two high schools. Its total student enrollment is comprised of 99.5 percent Latino, 90 percent low socioeconomic, 70 percent academically underserved, and 53 percent limited English proficient (Nodine, 2010). It is not the underrepresented student population that makes Hidalgo ISD notable; rather, it is the bold commitment it has made to prepare all its students from K–12th grade to attend college.

Committing to All

The Hidalgo local early college effort began when Daniel P. King, Hidalgo ISD superintendent, liked the idea of improving college opportunities for all its students. "Early college high schools were already outside the box," he said. "We wanted to go outside their box" (Hamilton, 2010). In partnership with nearby University of Texas–Pan American, the University of Texas System, and the Texas High School Project, they received approval for the "college for all" vision and a major grant from the Bill and Melinda Gates Foundation to become the nation's first comprehensive early college district.

As Hidalgo began its journey to become an early college district, educators borrowed or adapted many strategies from other early colleges.

Many challenges were unique to Hidalgo because of the emphasis on early college for all students. For over five years, Hidalgo educators and the community at large have learned much about what it takes a district to support every student to college success. They continuously assess and revise the design and practices to support students better and strengthen its sustainability.

Hidalgo collaborated with Jobs for the Future, a Boston-based organization that coordinates the nationwide initiative. They share and disseminate the lessons learned through an online toolkit. Hidalgo educators aim to inspire and instruct other school districts to adopt and adapt strategies that work in respective communities.

"No one is going to get away with saying, 'You can't find educated people in this region,'" Ed Blaha, former superintendent of the Hidalgo ISD, said. "Other people have this perception that if you live along the border region, you must not be really smart. If we don't dismiss those myths, nobody else is going to."

Of course, it's much easier to do when there is money available. "There is definitely a cost," said Blaha, who still finds himself confronting tough decisions as principal of Hidalgo Early College High School.

Daniel King said he hopes legislators realize that whatever the cost of fully financing public education is, "It costs less than having a lot of dropouts."

Blaha said, "Hidalgo will work through tough budgetary times as necessary. We've come this far." He added, "We can't go back."

Hidalgo has developed an infrastructure to transform the school district based on the following major components. It has

- developed rigorous course sequences,
- created comprehensive student support systems,
- organized strong parent engagement, and
- garnered robust college partnerships.

Hidalgo's graduation statistics boast a success revealing that two-thirds of the 2010 class graduated with at least one semester or more of college credit. Early College Program high schools are designed so students, underrepresented in higher education, can simultaneously earn a high school diploma and up to two years of college credit, tuition-free. Today, there are more than 230 Early College Programs nationwide. In Hidalgo, the search for grants to pay for students' books and materials is laborious, but they apply to foundations for all the needs of low-income, first-generation students.

Partnering With Local Colleges

From the beginning, Hidalgo educators established a close working relationship and a formal agreement with a college or university to develop a sustainable and effective early college program. Hidalgo ISD initiated partnership with a college presenting a partnership proposal to their school board.

Contacting college leaders is an important component. Eventually, the support of the college's president and the college's board will be crucial to ensure a strong commitment across the institution. It is also important to find supporters among faculty and the academic dean or provost. To establish working relationships at these levels, consider beginning by approaching contacts in dual enrollment programs and other programs serving first-generation college-goers. Such staff can facilitate additional relationships at the college. Ana Maria Rodriguez, senior vice provost of the University of Texas–Pan American states, "Both the school district and higher education need to embrace [Early College] and see it as our project together."

Hidalgo educators approached all meetings with a strong interest in learning about the college, its opportunities, and its expectations. Educators involved were also clear in describing their goals and identifying the resources they were committing to in support of student success. It is crucial that the school district and the college work together as equal partners, agreeing on the concepts and goals as they develop the partnership. Early discussions focused on the concept and goals of early college and its implications for the students and institutions. Securing support and commitment at the highest levels in the college and the district took high priority. Eventually, they formed a steering committee. The committee planned fees, instructors, transportation, books, and materials. They also discussed administrative and logistical challenges, from applications and financial aid to scheduling. Other crucial topics included academic issues and student supports, including course sequencing, instructional strategies, college readiness assessments, and academic advising.

The Hidalgo ISD prides itself in preparing their high school students for respective career pathways through college courses, and teachers support them in those courses. This involves hiring the right teachers that hold high expectations for students that are typically misunderstood or believed to be underachievers. If high school teachers seem uncertain about Latino college-going students' abilities, Hidalgo ISD then hires for summer positions, allowing them to audit the college courses while they also tutor students. Nicolás González, Associate Dean, South Texas

College, believes "that if students are given a chance, and you remove as many barriers as you can, they will astound you as to what they can do" (Hidalgo School District, 2011).

Direct lines of communication between and across the institutions are critical in facilitating the necessary planning and execution of programs. Some of the lines of communication connect across institutions, minimizing bureaucratic obstacles. For example:

- College president and the Hidalgo ISD superintendent set the vision and ensure the commitment of all the staff, families, and community.
- College dean/dual enrollment director and high school principals cut through bureaucracy, resolve challenges, and provide a consistent voice when logistical or procedural conflicts arise.
- Early college coordinator and high school counselors communicate across their respective institutions to understand the detailed rules, timelines, and procedures of college, including applications, financial aid, assessments, course selections, scheduling, and transcripts, as well as tracking student outcomes.
- College instructors and high school teachers establish ongoing communication, facilitating college faculty to learn effective instructional strategies to teach high school students.
- Ensuring smooth lines of communication may require a third party facilitator since the ongoing relationships need to sustain the various parts of the program. For this, Hidalgo solicited guidance from the Texas High School Project, a public–private alliance that plays an important role in building partnerships and ensuring good communication between the stakeholders. They have assisted Hidalgo's administration to develop a Memorandum of Understanding (MOU). For example, the MOU with South Texas College has helped Hidalgo build an early college infrastructure that holds down costs regarding tuition and instruction, transportation, and books.

CREATING A K–12 COLLEGE-GOING CULTURE IN HIDALGO ISD

Start young. Hidalgo schools reinforce the message of "college for all beginning in the early grades." At all levels, students and parents receive information about college and career options. Educators at Hidalgo do more than just talk. Classroom curricula, teaching methodology, and support services assist students to succeed in college classes.

Elementary Schools

From the first day of kindergarten, college becomes a reality in Hidalgo students' lives. Walking through the halls of their schools, students see college banners and displays surround them. Parents and community leaders visit classrooms to talk about their college experiences. Each classroom adopts a college, and students write to the institutions requesting pens, notebooks, and other items with the college logo. Elementary students meet with professors and wear college T-shirts to school on specially designated days. Teachers talk with parents about good study habits and other behaviors that build college success for their children. A senior girl with 49 credits at graduation time recalls, "[In] my family, nobody's ever been to college. My sister tried to go. She told me she didn't know what to do. She didn't know how to study. I want to prove that my family can do it" (Hidalgo School District, 2011).

Establishing positive attitudes that attending college is possible and necessary inspires students to envision an academic future giving meaning to their learning.

Middle Schools

The middle school is divided into three grade levels and each one into two teams. The school organizes trips for the teams not just to colleges but also to specific departments in the college. This expectation is that all students identify at least one area of academic interest and take pre-AP courses in that subject. Furthermore, all eighth graders attend a course designed to help them decide on a career. They identify both their own interests and the college options available to them at the high school. The eighth-grade counselor meets with each student toward the end of the year. They complete an educational plan, identifying college courses he or she might want to take in the future.

High Schools

Before entering ninth grade, students attend a math and English summer academy. They prepare for and take the Texas Higher Education Assessment, the statewide college readiness exam. Pre-advanced placement (pre-AP) and advanced placement (AP) courses comprise freshmen students' curricula. They advance academically such that most students begin to take college classes during their junior year.

The high school functions almost like a college campus. For example, students access the learning center/library to study after hours. Tutoring and other student supports take place before, during, and after school.

During the summer, about two-thirds of the students take college classes and earn credit recovery to accelerate. This way they are able to make up credits.

Connecting Rigorous With Intensive Academic Support

Ed Blaha believes that it is educators' responsibility to "make sure that by the time the kids leave us, that we've empowered them with the skills and the academic strength that are necessary for their next transition."

Rigor begins with teacher preparation. College knowledge is taught in a college success class. It provides tenth graders with skills to help students set up study groups for their college classes so that they can learn from and support one another. In all other classes, Hidalgo teachers are expected to generate high-level discussion and inquiry through problem solving and hands-on activities. Collaborative group work challenges students with diverse skill levels. Students master academic language through questioning, classroom discussions, daily writing assignments, and literacy groups. Teachers match secondary students to career tech or university-level math and English courses.

Accelerated learning and catch-up is also offered to students with special needs. Hidalgo educators expect all students to graduate from high school and attend college. Some tenth-grade students experience persistent difficulty passing the state assessments in language arts. They attend a Success Academy for intensive literacy instruction. English language learners, new to the United States, attend an accelerated program in English and math. And for students who are at risk of not graduating, Hidalgo Academy, a small alternative school, provides them with personalized instruction.

Individualized guidance minimizes the confusion many Latino students often feel trying to sort through college information, and this enables them to make informed decisions about their career options. Educational and career planning begins early. In Hidalgo, elementary school students learn about careers that are common in the Rio Grande Valley. Middle school students take a semester-long career awareness course, with several weeks dedicated to five career pathways. Counselors meet with eighth graders to help each select a career pathway and an educational plan for high school. By high school, students have already considered several occupations and the college admission process.

Redesigning Approaches for New Challenges

Former Superintendent Ed Blaha recognizes, "The greatest pitfall is to delay. Some thought we should go into this really slowly. My response is that we already serve the most underrepresented group of kids. They've heard enough 'not yet, no, let's wait.' When do we stop saying 'not yet' to these kids?" (Hidalgo School District, 2011).

Teachers, staff, and administrators try new approaches such as flexible class schedules, summer school activities, and workforce solutions to work as a team to help students succeed.

Class schedules in the middle school were changed to create an advisory period where all students receive tutoring and academic enrichment activities tailored to their needs. Likewise, the high school's eight-period schedule includes flexibility for tutoring during the school day. The schedule also provides common planning periods for academic departments, enabling teachers to share information about student interventions.

Summer school provides opportunities for all students from incoming to accelerated students. It operates the Bridge Academy for incoming ninth graders. It's an intensive four-week academy of accelerated instruction in math and language arts. College courses are offered for rising juniors and seniors, many of which are on college campuses.

Workforce solutions provide students with job experience, and the 21st Century program provides a range of activities from sports to tutoring. They also receive accelerated instruction and the opportunity for students below grade level to make up credits, especially for those who have not passed the state tests required for graduation.

Early College—Creating a Vision of Change

Hidalgo received a Bill and Melinda Gates Foundation grant through the Communities Foundation of Texas to become an Early College district. They also needed local resources to help plan. Networking with those who have experiences with Early Colleges—such as Jobs for the Future, the Texas High School Project, and the University of Texas—helped in planning and implementation. In communicating with their Board of Trustees, Hidalgo's Early College is transparent about their challenges and needs.

To succeed in providing every student an opportunity to excel academically, everyone in Hidalgo had to try new roles. Educators raised their expectations of students and took on greater roles for themselves in the process. Some ways that jobs change at the high school are as follows:

Principal—The high school principal focuses everyone on a way through conflict to resolution. For example, the principal is the on-the-ground leader in managing the partnerships with colleges. The principal must be a negotiator and communicator who can help others accept and bring about change, from college partners and teachers to parents and students. Every principal in the district works together to provide leadership toward early college for all.

Assistant principals—Each assistant principal is assigned to several academic and career-technical departments. They all meet regularly with the teachers in those departments to ensure they have the support needed to reach their instructional goals for early college, including aligning their curricula to those of college.

Teachers—Teachers receive training on a common set of instructional strategies that are effective in developing the deeper learning necessary to succeed in college classes. They meet as departments once a week to plan and align coursework between high school and college. Teachers also tutor before, during, and after school, and audit college classes with students on the college campus during summer.

Counselors—Counselors develop a master schedule that supports college course taking for students. They help students with high school planning, college planning, and career planning, and they motivate all students to take rigorous college courses. They also track student progress and grades across multiple institutions—including calculating grade point averages and class rankings. Counselors explain complex educational systems in comprehensible ways to parents and students. Principal Marilu states, "Navarro School counselors sit with each one individually and explain the application process. We tell them that tuition is waived. They just need to guarantee us that their child will be here every day. That's the guarantee we need from them" (Hidalgo School District, 2011).

Bus drivers, custodians, office clerks, food workers, and other staff—Bus drivers offer service at flexible times for students who stay after school for tutoring or college classes. Custodians and other staff are flexible in accommodating building use after school and on weekends. Food service workers also ensure that students have access to nutritious meals at appropriate times.

Aligning Courses and Career Paths

To align coursework between K–12 schools and colleges takes a great deal of negotiating because the secondary and postsecondary educational systems are organized and established independently. Hidalgo relied on strategies to build on the existing resources that others have developed. For example, teachers, counselors, and administrators visited other Early Colleges in Texas, including UT-San Antonio. Visits to Early College programs provides important context. Discussions grow from the sharing of course syllabi and assignments for entry-level college courses.

Building career pathways requires articulation with community college programs. Hidalgo works with college faculty and administrators to connect the high school's career pathways, including training programs offered by college partners. For example, the course sequences in business and marketing include introductory and advanced computer science classes, both of which provide students with high school and college credits.

The community college also provides high school seniors with remedial courses in math and English, which Hidalgo teachers teach with supervision from college faculty. Students who complete the courses are approved to take college-level math and English without taking the state assessment again. This program will save taxpayers the cost of providing remedial education in college for underprepared students.

THE FAMILIES' ROLE

Embracing Families and Communities as Resources

Hidalgo educators believe that parents, families, and the community comprise one of the most important components of their successful college culture and college-bound program. In fact, Hidalgo considers its parents and the community vital partners and allies in creating a strong support network for every student. In Hidalgo, most parents speak Spanish and have not had opportunities to attend college. Therefore, parent informational meetings usually take place bilingually in Spanish and English. Some of the ideas that foster strong communication between family, school, and community include:

- Educators attend local events and volunteer for civic duties.
- Schools host community events about college and careers.
- Schools invite parents into classrooms to talk about their careers.
- High school holds an annual career fair.
- Educators learn about neighborhood histories and demographics.
- Teachers tour the neighborhoods so they can see where their students live and where the parents work.

Shirley A. Reed, president of South Texas College, believes that the Rio Grande Valley is flourishing because "it is a community with something to prove." For too long, this region of the country has been seen as a place without educated people. The reality, however, is that there is a cost to efforts such as those that Hidalgo has initiated. To this, Blaha asserts, "We've come this far. We can't go back" (Hidalgo School District, 2011).

Going away to college: Most parents and community leaders were on board from the start. However, educators encountered resistance from some parents who were hesitant to allow their children to plan for the possibility of attending college away from home. One of the major issues for Hidalgo educators is to convince families that it advantages students to attend college even if it means leaving the area. To address this issue,

- educators regularly invite local alumni from UT-Austin, Texas A&M, and other universities to talk about the benefits of these kinds of institutions.
- the family's financial restrictions also concern them. Educators assist them in filling out financial aid forms. They encourage every senior to apply to at least one out-of-state college.
- counselors convene parents of students who have left home to go to college; they meet with parents who resist having their children leave home. Frank informative discussions between those with experience and those who have concerns expose the problem, resulting in clarifications that assist parents to make necessary cultural changes. Although Hidalgo does not report this third strategy in their Toolkit, it is a strategy that the Puente Project in Hayward, California implements.
- parent liaison position provides parents with easy access to a familiar contact; they created parent liaisons as staff positions at each school, which are funded through federal grants, including Title I.
- parents learn about study habits and other kinds of college knowledge associated with success in college.
- parents organize district-wide meetings. The programs include school-related topics (graduation requirements, colleges, scholarships), as well as skill building in areas identified by parents, such as drug awareness, border safety, the H1N1 virus, and parenting.

Parent education is a high priority because it completes the full circle so that students have strong role models for educational success within their own families and neighborhoods. Parents also attend academies for encouragement to pursue their own educational goals. The academies offer adult education in ESL, GED classes, computer instruction, and preparation for the Texas Higher Education Assessment (THEA), which is the statewide college readiness test. The classes are funded from several sources, including federal grants (Title I, Title III, and stimulus funding), philanthropic grants, and local funds.

Coping With Stressful Academic Demands

Parents are often unfamiliar with the challenges of college course taking while in high school, and when their children need support with difficult courses. The high school has a policy to encourage students to take AP courses and discourage them from dropping those courses prematurely, before they have adjusted to the high expectations of these courses. Educators recommend to parents that if their children complain about academic challenges that they should listen and also work with the respective teacher or counselor to resolve the issue.

PUENTE PROJECT

The Bridge

Puente means "bridge" in Spanish. In California, since the 1980s Puente has existed in community colleges and a few years later high schools adopted the program. Puente operates at 33 high school and 59 community college sites. It consists of three braided components: writing, counseling, and mentoring. The Puente staff train high school and community college teams to implement a program of accelerated writing instruction, intensive academic counseling, and mentoring/leadership training by members of the respective community sites across the California. Puente operates out of the Office of the President of the University of California headquartered in Oakland. It supports underserved students, primarily Latinos in 35 state high schools by presenting a core subject, such as preparatory English, and supplemental learning in a culturally relevant context.

This interdisciplinary approach provides a focused, sustained, and engaging learning environment for students. This model and approach provides students with individual, culturally sensitive, academic, and career counseling designed to help each of them graduate and enroll in a four-year institution. Currently, Puente benefits approximately 14,000 students annually. It is open to all students. However, Latino students generally comprise the largest group participating in Puente.

Program Divisions

Three divisions define Puente—writing, counseling, and mentoring for ninth-and tenth-grade students. Each provides critical skills, enabling students to reach college.

Writing—Within the framework of college prep curriculum, writing classes begin with a developmental writing course, followed by a college transfer-level English composition course. Students remain in writing classes with the same professor for one academic year. Teachers emphasize rigor while creating a supportive environment. A teacher in a southern California Puente program describes the importance of creating a *familia* (family) culture in his classroom. "Educators need to approach teaching . . . with total passion, making high demands, providing plenty of encouragement, and emphasizing a shared sense of community. . . . Bringing my students together as a family increases their chances of success—the assistance and encouragement they get from each other helps anchor some that might otherwise be distracted from their long-term dreams by short-term temptations. . . . Some of my students feel like they do not belong in the academic world, that reading and writing are for students who look different or come from different ethnic backgrounds. To have lasting effect on underserved students, I must effect a paradigm shift on them: They need to think of themselves as writers" (Turner, 2008 pp. 16–17).

Counseling—Lack of adequate counseling services in elementary and high schools has disadvantaged underrepresented students. Hiring qualified counselors poses a challenge for programs such as Puente. They need to be educators informed and experienced in working with academically challenged students. Counselors also need to build trust with the students served (Oakes, 1995). This Puente component has helped students succeed on their way to college. Counselors arrange visits to college campuses and informational field trips for students to become informed about their career goals.

Mentoring—The mentoring component is a vital link between the local community and the school program. Mentors help students increase leadership skills and community involvement. Students are encouraged to return to their community as leaders and mentors to future generations. They are motivated to reach their academic and personal potential by obtaining college degrees—the one thing that their parents did not have the opportunity to attain.

As a student at the University of California at Santa Cruz in 2009, Devina credits the Puente Project for steering her to college. "I felt like I could do it because they believed in me, and it helped me believe in myself." Devina shares her story on how Puente helped her grow in confidence and skills to get to college. Her working-class, first-generation parents grew up in immigrant families from Mexico and Nicaragua. "In my family, it was about getting a job and making a living, not pursuing goals of higher education."

By her sophomore year at James Logan High School, Devina set her sights on an undergraduate degree. Though she struggled with math and faced challenges in her personal life, Lopez finished high school (Yeung, 2009). "My counselor was a huge, huge part of my high school life," Devina says. "She advised us on classes to take, and she would always check up on us."

Devina participated in a community of motivated peers. She felt the support to obtain resources she didn't know how to access. The Program also helped her navigate her way to graduation and college. "They were a huge support and influence on how I view myself and my potential," she says of her Puente friends, teacher, and counselor. They gave her the confidence to ignore negative labels such as *inferior* or *disadvantaged*. As a Latina student, she was all too familiar with these stereotypes. However, Puente served as her safety net and encouraged her strong feelings about herself.

Parent and Family Engagement

The power of parental engagement has been documented widely. And the Puente Project has observed its influence in preparing students for college. Gandara (2011) reports, "86 percent of principals, head counselors and English department chairs at Puente high schools said their schools have been changed by Puente, largely due to huge increases in parent involvement." Puente counselors and instructors work to acknowledge the social and cultural identities of students' families and to integrate those identities into the program. Counselors are encouraged to involve family members or guardians as active participants in the high school program and to provide them with opportunities for leadership by involving them in the planning and execution of Puente activities. Puente instructors create and foster a *familia*-like environment to provide students with the support and motivation likely to enable them to succeed in furthering their educational goals. Parent and family involvement and participation contribute to these ends.

GEAR UP

The transition from middle to high school requires a great deal from the school and from community groups outside of school. GEAR UP stands for "Gaining Early Awareness and Readiness for Undergraduate Programs." The program partners with schools to support students during this phase of their schooling. Middle school student Carlos's experience in the Massachusetts GEAR UP prefaces how it shapes his hopes and aspirations.

My mom never went to college and she pushed me to get into GEAR UP so I can have a chance. She really supports me. Now I know I have a chance. It is a lot of fun participating in all the activities and spending time with family and friends. And I like that I'm learning too. (GEAR UP, 2012)

GEAR UP serves all students who need assistance. However, the Latinos comprise the largest group. Students begin the program in the seventh grade and it follows the cohort through high school (U.S. Department of Education, 2003). Nationally, it operates 237 partnerships where schools partner with the state or higher education institutions, serving over 200,000 students. The federal government provides six-year grants to states and local partnerships to operate in high-poverty middle and high schools. The program funds are also used to provide college scholarships to low-income students.

States offer schools a competitive six-year matching grant that must include both an early intervention component designed to increase college attendance and success and raise the expectations of low-income students and a scholarship component. Partnership grants are competitive six-year matching grants that must support an early intervention component and may support a scholarship component intended to increase college attendance and success and raise the expectations of low-income students.

The positive aspect of GEAR UP is that its services are not remedial. Rather, it focuses on advancing students forward, meaning that they support students' advanced academic work. Typically, the program encourages students who need remedial classes to seek support from other places. Each school program determines which services students receive according to need. Thus, every program differs slightly or significantly from others.

As defined by GEAR UP, partnerships involve the schools working with local organizations, businesses, colleges, and faith groups. These types of partnerships haven't been as successful as the school partnerships with the state. The partnerships that work best are those that provide educational programs or services such as occupational skills training or a software program.

In addition, a few projects also engage social welfare agencies already actively involved in participating communities. Key partners, including colleges and school districts, rely heavily on GEAR UP staff, including project directors or site coordinators. Many of these positions have shifted to local participating schools. Principals play an increasingly central role, making the school a more key figure in the operations (Hickok, 2003).

GEAR UP is designed with strategies for encouraging high-risk middle and high school students to prepare for college. A typical project has a full-time director and possibly one other full-time staff member from the local community. Oklahoma GEAR UP is one example: Partnering with 23 school districts, it implements sustainable practices to help create college-bound communities (GEAR UP, 2012).

The promise of GEAR UP's partnership with public schools is evident in the success of its students. In the Jamaica Plain, Boston area, college graduate Daisy recalls her supportive academic environment during the years that she participated in GEAR UP in her community.

I was in the third grade when I wrote a story that won a prize in my school and I got to attend a workshop and share my story with others part of a wider competition. So, I've always known that writing was my thing.

I was in the seventh grade when a teacher told me that there was a tutoring program that I could benefit from. I was a good student, but I always wanted to learn more. I convinced my friend to go with me because I was a very shy Salvadorian kid. We enjoyed going after school because we liked our tutor. She was a college student and she gave us lot of attention and help. I asked her lots of questions about what college was about because I had heard from my parents that I should take advantage of every opportunity to get a good education. And I didn't know what college was about except that I should go, so my tutor was very good about sharing her experience. At the end of middle school, we received a certificate for attending. My tutor also brought me a gift bag. She gave me candy and a guardian angel. I loved it. By then my friend had stopped going with me. I felt sad when she lost interest. Our director, Carmen, called her and I called her too, but she got too involved with boys. So when she received a certificate too, I was angry and told her, 'You don't deserve the certificate.' It was my way of getting even with her for abandoning me. Later in high school, she dropped out.

In high school, I continued attending GEAR UP. We met in the room next to the childcare. Yes, at least 40 percent of the girls in the school were pregnant. I appreciated the workshops on how to apply for college and financial aid. Although I didn't attend tutoring very much because I felt confident that I was doing well academically, I did go on a weekend science outing to Maine. We also visited the university of Maine, where the dean of admissions talked to us about the university. Then he said, 'You kids wouldn't be able to attend our university because you are urban students and we only take excellent students.' We all gasped and Carmen stepped in and told him that we were excellent students and would qualify to attend any university. He didn't insult us anymore, but the damage was done. Since I didn't want to go to a rural school, I didn't take his undermining comments seriously. There are too many people out there that don't believe we can make it simply because of where students live and their looks.

In spite of her supportive parents, teachers, and her own enthusiasm for learning throughout her schooling, Daisy faced negative attitudes about her academic ability. Besides the academic support and the college application process, reassuring students of their potential is an equally important feature of GEAR UP.

Daisy shared that GEAR UP was supportive even into her college years. Although the program was not officially at the university, the director, Carmen, tracked her progress and offered whatever assistance she could to help Daisy deal with some very difficult health problems that developed. Daisy was a part of the Robert E. McNear Scholars group. In addition to her regular coursework, they had to write a lengthy research paper each year and commit to go on to graduate school. Daisy felt quite stressed working 20 hours a week and taking a full-time course load and maintaining a high GPA to keep her scholarship while dealing with family pressures because her parents lost their jobs. With the support of GEAR UP, she graduated with her B.A. degree and will soon begin her graduate program in writing.

REFLECTION

Making school–university–nonprofit organization partnerships integrate community strengths into the school program and give elementary and secondary students opportunities and experiences they otherwise would not have. The school, the community organizations, and most importantly, the students all benefit from these efforts.

BEST PRACTICES FOR EDUCATORS

Successful Approaches

Hidalgo School District utilizes these activities to create a college culture:

- *Seek grants for curriculum development.* Hidalgo writes state-level grants for curriculum alignment and development across systems, particularly between high school and middle school. For example, these grant opportunities, some of which include professional development, have paid summer stipends for high school and middle school teachers to align their curricula.
- *Summer employment.* Hidalgo pays high school teachers to tutor groups of students who are taking college classes. Teachers also attend college classes with the students in the mornings, and often establish ongoing working relationships with the faculty.
- *Communication between high school and college faculty.* Hidalgo removes any administrative barrier such as e-mail and Internet restriction that may prevent them from communicating with college faculty.

Tip

This list is adapted from GEAR UP. The website provides online assistance to students from fifth through seventh grade with tips for studying. Educators can utilize this guideline in their classroom or student counseling sessions. See website for other tips: www.okhighered.org/gearup/students/planning-college.shtml.

Studying for a Test

1. Start early! An "all-nighter" is the least effective way to study for a test.

2. Schedule several study sessions before a test. Repetition is the key to remembering.

3. Attend class, especially before a big test. Ask questions about the test. Find out as much as possible: What will it cover? What type will it be—essay, multiple choice, or true or false? How much time will you have to complete the test?

4. Learn the important information. Here are some activities to help: Using your class notes and your textbook, make flash cards with facts, definitions, people, dates, events, lists, and so forth.

5. The act of writing the information on the cards will help you remember it. Each time you go through the stack of cards, you are transferring the information from your short-term memory into your long-term memory.

6. If you learn better by listening, study with a friend or family member who can ask you the questions or give the answers aloud to yourself.

7. Don't forget charts, diagrams, and captions to pictures in your textbook. They can contain lots of valuable information.

8. Use memory devices for learning lists or parts of something.

9. For items that do not have to be remembered in any particular order, take their first letters and see if you can arrange them into a word or an easily remembered order.

10. For example, the first letters of the Great Lakes spell HOMES.

11. Study with a friend—compare notes, ask each other questions, do flash cards together, and discuss themes that would make good essay questions.

Play the role of your teacher.

1. Make up the most difficult test you can and test yourself until you know the answers.

2. Use visuals to help you learn—invent charts, diagrams, trees, and drawings to help you remember.

3. Study past quizzes.

4. Study until the answers come to you easily.

Here are a few tips to help you deal with math anxiety:

1. It's okay if you don't know how to solve a problem. Mathematicians confront this every day.

2. Think of a math problem as an interesting puzzle that you are going to solve.

3. Just like a crossword puzzle, nothing is at stake in your solution, except the joy of coming to grips with the problem!

4. Don't expect to solve a problem instantly. Take all the time you need. Logical thinking cannot be done on a timetable.

5. Don't expect to remember every tool needed to solve a problem. Right in the middle of a solution, you may need to look up information or examples to help you.

6. Find your happy math place. You use math more than you think throughout the day—shopping, sports. You did it then. You can do it now.

Get help if you need it.

1. Maybe you have a family member or friend who can help or maybe you need help from a tutor. Either way, it's better to ask for help than to never learn the skills.

2. Watch the Math Path DVD. Order a free copy at OKcollegestart .org.

3. *Don't wait until the last minute!* However, if you did put it off and now you need some *tips on the go* . . . here they are: Get a good night's sleep the night before the test. Avoid caffeinated or sugary drinks before taking the test as they can make you jittery. Eat a balanced meal. *No* doughnuts! Wear comfortable clothing. If you get stuck on a question, mark it and move on. You can come back to it later. If the test permits, do a memory check. Jot down important formulas or information on a piece of scrap paper.

The Math Path

Fifth-Through Seventh-Grade Math Activity Related to Career Planning

In the DVD program, the Math Path, examples are given of how different careers would be affected in a world without math. Here are some suggested problems for students to solve to see how math is used in various careers and its importance in daily life: www.okhighered.org/gearup/educators/math-path-worksheet%202.pdf.

The following materials are meant to be used in conjunction with the GEAR UP DVDs indicated. If you haven't seen the DVDs, you can order them online. Just fill out the materials request form: http://www .okhighered.org/gearup/gearup-college-prep-materials. Other materials and activities are available in different subjects for students up to twelfth grade. Materials are also available in Spanish.

College Planning With Parents

8

A PARENT'S EARLY DREAM FOR COLLEGE

Sylvia, her husband, and three children live in a suburb. For Sylvia, parenting her three children to succeed academically was her life's mission. Guiding her two older children, Saul in middle school and Sonia in high school, keeps her attending frequent school and community meetings, and staying current on what her children need to succeed in their respective schools. She recounts how difficult it is to juggle her family life and work while staying connected with her children and their school needs but how gratifying it is to be living her life's dream. Sylvia's story moves us through her efforts to get engaged in her children's school in their early years and how that became her impetus to ensure that they got on the right track to college.

(Translated from Spanish) When I was growing up in Mexico and had to quit school to take care of my mother who was ill for a long time, I promised myself that when I grew up and had my own children that I would do everything in my power to ensure that they would get the best education possible.

When I married and my husband and were able to immigrate, I was so happy because I knew that my children would be born here and they would have the educational opportunities would make my dream come true.

When my children were young, I loved reading to them at home and teaching them everything I remember learning during the very few years I spent in school in Mexico. The funny part about it was that when they began school, at first it didn't occur me to go to the school unless the teachers called me for parent conferences. Then one day when my son, Saul, was in fourth grade he got into a fight with some boys and I went to find out why this had been allowed to happen. At that time, the teacher told me that she wasn't surprised because he was a problem student. I was furious that this was the first report of these circumstances that I had heard. I asked her what I could do to change this situation and she said that he had to work harder and pay attention. I told her about everything we did at home to encourage our children to do their schoolwork and stay healthy so they can do well in school. She said that his behavior had to improve or she'd have him removed from her classroom. I assured her that my husband and I would do everything possible to help Saul, but I told her that I needed more regular reports from her about his work and his behavior.

The teacher's reports came home regularly and they were all very negative. Our talks with Saul at home were very different and we wanted to believe that he wasn't lying to us. After all, his homework was getting done and he seemed to want to go to school. He felt that he was getting along with others. When I met with the teacher about the difference between her accounts and his, she accused him of lying and said that it was part of his pattern. I didn't know what to do because her attitude toward him seemed so negative. I told a friend of mine at church about the situation and she told me to talk with the school principal and request that he be moved from her class. I was embarrassed and asked her to go with me. My friend helped me to ask the questions and to help my son. He had to stay in the same class, but I figured out that I had to move him from school. I started talking to other neighbors and parents of my children's friends. He was able to get into another school that was a bit farther, but I didn't care as long as he could do better there.

It worked. His grades improved in the new school. The school also had a bilingual parent group that I started attending and learned so much about how to help my children to get good opportunities and plan for a good career. From other parents, I started to hear about their children in high school needing advanced classes to get to college. That was something I needed to understand because my daughter Sonia was getting into high school soon.

So I began talking to him about going to college because he was a good student and had lots of dreams about being a scientist. I got busy asking the school lots of questions about the classes he should take and how he could get into those classes. I was like a mother possessed, learning everything possible and making Saul and Sonia, my older daughter, learn along with me because it was about their future. I became so informed about how much it takes to prepare children to get to the right classes and what college was about that I pushed for Sonia to get to attend a new magnet school that was opening up in a neighboring school district. The school was dedicated to prepare students for college. By the time Saul was ready for middle school, I found out that he could apply to get into a good charter school, which was near the magnet high school. In my private moments, I dreaded all of the driving to take them and pick them up from school, not to mention all of the meetings that I had to attend because both schools insisted on many hours of parent involvement. I just prayed for strength and lots of patience.

Finally, I had my children in good schools. My dream had come true. I just didn't know that it was going to mean so much work on my part. The work part didn't bother me, but I just kept wondering how other parents got all of this information that I had to figure out on my own.

Sylvia navigates through the odyssey that many Latino parents travel. She underscores the importance of clear, consistent, and continuous communication about early academic performance between educators and families—the two main institutions that Latino students need on their side from the minute they enter through the kindergarten door to the time they walk through the door of their college of choice. Connecting across the home/school border happens when both educators and parents learn about each other's culture. That is, what happens in the school is of as critical importance to parents as what happens in the home is of significance to educators. When parents are not as visible in their children's schools, educators often believe that they are indifferent about education. This couldn't be farther from the truth. Often when families live in low-socioeconomic conditions, parents work more than two jobs trying to keep shelter over their children's heads and food on the table, so they may not get to school meetings as needed. They may also not have the experience of formal education, making it difficult to stay current on their children's academic performance throughout their schooling career. Nevertheless, work in Latino communities (Delgado Gaitan, 2001, 2004) shows that regardless of their inexperience with schools, parents care about their children's learning. They want them to succeed in school and prepare themselves for a career that will move them into better economic standing.

Latino parents have just as much strength as they have questions about the schooling process. Some of their strengths include a strong work ethic and communication in two languages, which they share with their children. Parents value respect, authority, and *educación* in high regard. *Educación* translates in broader perspective than "education." Latinos expect an educated person to be disciplined and behave properly. Respect and authority go hand in hand as parents believe that children respect their teachers and other adults as well as themselves. Resilience describes how many Latino parents cope with the stress in navigating a different culture and language to understand how to support their children on the road to college. Along the way, they encounter frequent failures and strong support systems as they collaborate with educators and other parents.

These strengths are key springboards for engaging parents in the school to address a college culture for their children from the early years till their admission to college. In no way should parents let go after their children are admitted into college.

Research suggests that parents of Mexican descent exert a positive influence on their children's college aspirations. Yet a void exists in the college choice and application process (Ceja, 2006; Gonzalez, Stoner, & Jovel, 2003). Educators and parents must collaborate throughout all the grades to ensure that students have the most important adults in their corner as they make decisions about the college.

FIVE Cs OF FAMILY ENGAGEMENT

To sustain Latino parent engagement in schools, educators need to establish well-founded conditions in which to build an effective partnership. The most important elements that socially construct true mutual trust include commitment, communication, consistency, cooperation, and collaboration. One of the most important questions that educators want answered is how to get Latino parents to attend any meeting or event. They attend when they feel included and believe that their voice is valued. They need to have a voice in the topic being discussed. Schools may need to reach out to community groups where Latino parents create a strong active core. It can be churches, community centers, or medical clinics. A small group of active parents providing input on the agenda for school meetings is an initial step that can bring in other parents. Successful schools attract large groups of Latino parents when they provide information about practical needs in their daily lives such as information about obtaining health insurance. Another way that schools communicate with large groups of Latino parents is by providing English classes. These settings provide an attentive audience for ongoing communication and an opportunity to involve parents in organizing committees, workshops, and ways of staying connected with other parents.

Commitment

Engaging Latino families in the schools requires more than holding occasional informational meetings. A commitment to a systematic collaboration between the two begins in district-level policy. When formulating a parent involvement policy at the central office or school level, parents need to be involved in the process. Parents' input in their role makes parent involvement more effective because it connotes a two-way communication where both educators and parents understand and agree on their rights and responsibilities. Including a parent engagement statement in school policy raises the family–school partnership to strong educational platform.

Communication

Bilingual written correspondence should go home with students every day. That is a valuable step in reaching Latino parents. However, parents often prefer to communicate face-to-face with educators because some of the language in written correspondence is unfamiliar to them. Comprehensible language means using terminology that parents comprehend. Technical educational language needs to be unpacked so that parents understand the concepts clearly. Receiving information is only one aspect of communication. If schools expect parents to participate in the discussion of the issues or to take action, both written and verbal communication needs to be bilingual, clear, comprehensible, and constant.

Consistency

To execute an effective parent engagement plan, parents and educators need to create a continuous system of communication. The only way to create real communication between parents and educators is to establish a sound foundation of ongoing continuous exchange through written, verbal, and technological means. Too often educators wait until there is a crisis or urgent need to contact Latino parents. Reaching out to parents needs to be much more than a one-time encounter. Using crisis to reach out to the community accomplishes the goal of providing information on that specific matter. However, only consistency of communication establishes a trusting report with Latino parents. Bridging the home and school divide means developing an ongoing dialogue about the myriad of issues that arise in children's schooling from kindergarten through high school, particularly with parents who have little knowledge of how schools operate and what is expected of their students and of them.

Cooperation

Educators need to work together in developing viable parent engagement programs. Successful schools or programs have programs where teachers, counselors, and administrators combine forces with each other to fashion a systematic program to relate to Latino families and the community. Effective parent engagement programs offer to the community the strengths and professional expertise of teachers, counselors, and administrators (Auerback, 2004).

Collaboration

Schools often confine their outreach to Latino families to involve only the specific parents of the students in their schools. Certainly, that is the most important target population. However, in each community, certain agencies, foundations, or organizations that support the Latino families make important partners in the dialogue with parents. Collaborations between Latino support groups can often support the parents and educators in bringing about wide-scale community changes to empower Latino parents in working closer with their children, enabling them to succeed academically on their way to college.

In some school districts where schools are geographically removed from the community, parents prefer to meet with educators in places closer to their homes. Schools utilize community organizations that the families are familiar with.

PARENTS WANT TO KNOW

In a northern California community, Mr. Soto expressed how much he wanted to learn to help his children in school. In his words, "Ignorance makes one believe that strength is in the body, not in the mind. When one thinks that way, we do not stop and think and negotiate with others. But that's the reason we need to talk with counselors and others who can help us understand our children's educational needs." This is an interesting statement because some Latino parents who work in agriculture, construction, housekeeping, or factories doing important work that requires different forms of intelligence as well as physical strength feel that they are not as intelligent as other parents whose work takes place in offices. Mr. Soto's call for engaging with others to transcend the void of information sets the stage for major questions, specifically about getting students to college.

How to finance college: Often before learning how to apply for college, Latino parents want to know how they can help their child finance college since many families live in households with limited financial resources. In the face of serious economic decline, Latino students are even more inclined than usual to prefer entering the labor market after completing high school as opposed to attending college and pursuing a career (Price, 2010). Parents want to know how to access the sources and how to complete the reams of forms required in the process.

How to apply for college: Where to begin can be overwhelming for many parents. They want all the information as well as a real hands-on step-by-step class on how to complete the forms. Typically students don't get the details of the application process until the high school years, but if parents receive some of this information in the early years, they can learn about entrance requirements.

What are the best colleges: Once parents commit to the process of helping their children attend college, they become interested in where children can get the best education. This decision is bound up with whether their child can qualify for the college that would be considered the "best." Therefore, ways to respond to this is multifold. For parents of students in the early years, they can use the information to motivate their children to succeeding academically to get to the best college of their choice.

About daily life in college: Few things matter as much to Latino parents as their children leaving home even if it is to attend college. One of the paramount questions they want to learn about is, what goes on in colleges? How do students spend their time when they're not in class? How safe are the living quarters? How often can parents visit them? How often can they leave campus to visit the family? As protective as parents may seem for raising these questions, their concerns stem from their inexperience with college life.

Schools Collaborating With Parents

The recommendations below are based on some of the successful educator/parent engagement approaches of engaging Latino parents about the college culture. Some of them need to begin in the early grades. Other strategies described here span all the grade levels from K–12.

- Start early.

Parents who participated in the Pacific High School project were grateful for the information they received, but they regretted not having college information earlier. Parent engagement, including meetings with educators and support groups among parents needs to begin as soon as students start school. The modes of connection as well as the content of the information discussed between parents and educators differs somewhat because the needs are different for the age groups. Nevertheless, starting as early as kindergarten, parent meetings and information need to address good study skills, good healthy habits (sleeping, eating, making friends), and good planning activities between parents and children regarding personal interest and possible careers. Strong beginnings build on each other, and as students move up the grades, the college culture becomes more familiar until it becomes something that isn't questioned by the time students reach the application process time high school.

- Communicate in parents' language.

Earlier in this chapter, I discussed much of what needs stating about the use of language in connecting with Latino parents. It is insufficient to translate information to Spanish because parents may be unable to understand the content of the communication. That is, it's not only what language is used; it is what is said in that language that matters. Much of what parents want to communicate with educators deals with personal feelings and questions about their children in school. Not assuming that educators know how parents think or feel opens the communication to a two-way interaction. Ensuring trust and confidence between parents and educators needs to occur in the parents' language, but it may also need to happen face-to-face in a setting that is familiar or comfortable to families. Hiring community liaisons or coordinators to communicate personally with parents enriches the ongoing communication between families and educators. Dispensing information is one-way communication, but listening to parents about their feelings, ideas, and needs in their language constitutes two-way exchange.

- Organize convenient meetings.

Educators may think that large informational parent meetings mean that many parents care about the topic at hand and large groups may feel safe for parents because they attend with others, but they are not conducive to meaningful interaction between educators and parents. When discussing intimate topics such as their children going to college, a topic that can be emotionally charged for many reasons, face-to-face meetings need to be small and comfortable for parents to share informally without intimidation. The best settings may be convenient and familiar places in the community rather than the school.

- Talk about college.

Latino parents relate to learning about school matters through personal narratives that others share about their experience. Many programs succeed in keeping parents informed by inviting local professionals with similar experience as the community they address. Sharing their personal family and college experience helps Latino families put a personal face to something as distant from their expertise as planning for college.

- Feature college culture information continuously in meetings, conferences, and communications with parents.

Presenting the facts about what the college application process is and the deadlines for college application does not make college information sessions meaningful to parents. Latino parents may have good intentions for assisting their children through the college socialization process, but the fact that they are not as familiar with the need to keep the subject up front constantly means that parents need encouragement to talk about college at parent meetings. Frequently engaging parents to read about and discuss the broader college culture, including students' academic standing, college visits, mentors, and adhering to the application deadlines, reminds the family of the importance and the activities that need to be continuously monitored.

- Present general information and address parents' personal concerns.

Parents want to understand everything that's involved in shepherding students to college starting in the early years. Much of the information about socializing students is somewhat strategic such as where families can obtain financial aid for college. However, some issues that parents want to address come from a deeper emotional place such as why students need to leave home to attend college. During meetings, the more intimate questions can get addressed in small groups where parents can share openly their concerns and converse with an informed and thoughtful professional who is culturally aware and understands the community.

- Allow parents to meet individually with school and college representatives.

Latino parents sometimes prefer to speak privately to authority figures. Therefore, personal conferences with educators enables parents to pose questions of a more delicate nature or topics that they may feel embarrassed to ask in larger groups.

- Assist parents to support each other through the college planning process.

Important changes in the Latino community occur in the context of supportive groups. In environments with people like themselves, parents are inclined to support one another in thinking, deciding, and taking action on things that may be new or feel uncomfortable for them such as helping their children apply for college or allowing their children to leave home for college. Increasing the college attendance in the Latino community is one cultural change that requires positive reinforcement not only for authority figures they respect but also family members like themselves.

- Acknowledge the barriers to college access for Latinos and encourage parents to learn about educational inequality.

Raising consciousness about political realities can help mobilize parents to organize themselves and learn ways to connect with other communities to change educational policies and processes that impede Latino students getting to college. In some communities, parent empowerment is of great consequence to educators'/parents' college culture informational meetings. In this next section, parents in a San Francisco, California school illustrate the power of commitment on the part of parents as they collaborate with the school and community organizations.

PARTNERING WITH FAMILIES AND COMMUNITIES

In 2009, the University of California, Berkeley, Center for Educational Partnerships through Gail Kaufman's office developed the Believing the College Dream Program and Curriculum to support fourth- through eighth-grade students to succeed in school and chart their way to college while empowering parents and communities. The Believing the Dream project was sponsored by the Educational Credit Management Corporation (ECMC) foundation. Applying the Believing the College Dream Parent Leadership Project/Platicas-Community Conversations in schools is a joint project of UC Berkeley Center for Educational Partnerships and Mission Graduates, a community-based organization in San Francisco sponsored by the Zellerbach Family Fund. Although the curriculum is designed for all underrepresented students, the curriculum was translated into Spanish for Latino parents.

For Latino parents to assist their young children in building academic skills and to participate in a college culture in school and in their community, they need a curriculum to empower them. The goal is to learn how to make decisions in tandem with schools with respect to creating a college culture. This also includes learning about the many resources available to their children and how they can access them in order to qualify for college. Part of the students' lessons involve them working with their parents and family members on college-going activities.

ECMC, the Center for Educational Partnerships, and the Mission Graduates Organization in San Francisco partnered to train Latino parent leaders in four schools, who in turn use the Believing the College Dream Curriculum to teach other parents.

Platicas at César Chavez School

In 2010, Kaufman's office in the Center for Educational Partnerships conducted pre and post survey's administered to English-/Spanish-speaking parents in Bay Area communities where staff presented college knowledge parent workshops on financial aid, college systems/college requirements (Kaufman, 2010). The results on a sample of 5 out of 22 survey questions indicate the importance of parent education curriculum (see end of chapter section).

César Chavez Elementary School was the setting of an empowering parent training that parents agreed to attend and the school hosted on campus. The six-month Platicas Program covered a range of topics: (1) importance of college, (2) types of colleges, (3) financing college, (4) development of academic skills, (5) making successful transitions, and (6) utilizing community resources. ECMC, the Center for Educational Partnerships, and the Mission Graduates Organization trained four parents over a three-month period to conduct the Platica parent trainings. All training was conducted in Spanish and their curriculum was translated to Spanish. Their verbal and written interactions were in Spanish and translated for this chapter.

The room was set up with six round tables, each sitting about eight persons. On each table was a large board with pictures, statistics, a school cheer, and other general information in Spanish about a different college.

Before the meeting began, two parents talked. Daniela, one of the parent leaders, commented to another woman, "The topic today is the most important of all because we need to help our children excel academically." The other parent agreed, "That's why I'm here because I want to help my daughter as much as possible and sometimes I don't really know how."

The fourth Platica meeting began at 9:00 a.m. with two parent leaders up front posting three large sheets. One sheet included some review points of the third Platica on financing a college education. Matilde asked the parents, *"Besides the money you've saved, what are the types of financing available to students if they apply for them?"* Several hands went up and she called on a few of them to answer the question. Following a few other review questions, Matilde, one of the women leaders, asked the 25 parents—24 women and 1 man—in attendance to review their group rules. They were: raise hand, keep confidentiality, put phones on vibrate, pay attention, and be respectful. Matilde engaged the parents with an opening line, *"The information that we're discussing this morning is like vitamins to a body. We're the bodies and the information is our vitamin. If we have a strong body we can help our children to develop a strong body too."* Parents smiled and nodded. Matilde then introduced Daniela as the person who would continue with the day's topic.

Daniela stepped up and led with a question, *"How many of you liked doing homework when you were in school?"* About half of the parents raised their hands. Others mumbled that they didn't like it because it was boring. Daniela continued her presentation with PowerPoint slides. The topics went systematically from how parents can participate in helping their children with their homework by communicating with their children about the work even if they cannot actually assist them. Setting a strict scheduled time and place were discussed because some parents felt that their children preferred to listen to music while they studied. Daniela and other parents chimed in about the fact that children learn differently and the important thing was to keep an eye on their children that they actually were getting their work done carefully and accurately if they preferred to listen to music.

Throughout the presentation, Daniela engaged parents on every topic with well-framed questions that got them to think and express their thoughts about topics, including recognizing importance of completing homework, becoming informed on how homework is corrected and valued by teachers, designating a space and minimizing distractions, providing appropriate resources, getting students organized, supervising homework, and communicating, coordinating, and cooperating with educators. Among the many comments parents made was one woman who shared, *"I used to struggle with my daughter doing homework. She resisted for a long time and I was very frustrated. Then I changed the way I talked to her. I used to tell her, 'Do your homework.' Now I tell her, 'Let's do homework.' Now she jumps right up and we start doing it together."*

On the topic of the importance of grades, one parent said, "I think grades are especially important for Latino students because many of them are in EL classes and need to be reclassified to get into more advanced English classes. But many don't get reclassified because we don't push our children too get good grades and push the teachers to reclassify them. So it's important for us as parents to stay in touch with the teachers. They need to know that we want our children to get reclassified and get into the advanced classes that will prepare them to get into college."

For the one-and-a-half hour of the meeting, parent leaders, with the assistance of Gerber from Mission Graduates, the coordinator between parents and the school, conducted a highly energized participatory discussion about the topic of the ECMC developed curriculum. At the end of the meeting, parents filled out an evaluation form, then parents at every table took turns chanting the "school chant" of the college that was on the chart on top of their table.

When this group of parents completes this initial six-part training at César Chavez, parents will be selected to convene another set, or training. The missing piece of the ECMC college culture curriculum at the time the parents were receiving training is the fourth- through eighth-grade student curriculum that teachers would teach to their students in the classroom. Parents expressed a desire for teachers to work along with them in preparing and supporting their children for college.

Empowered Parent Leaders

Before Daniela and Matilde trained to become parent leaders for presenting the Believing the College Dream Curriculum, they had their respective experiences in the way that they recognized the importance of becoming involved in their children's education.

Matilde, a single mother of a 10-year-old son in fourth grade with learning disabilities, describes her relationship with her son's school.

(Translated from Spanish) Because my son has a speech disability, I've had to pay attention in the kind of education that he was receiving from the beginning when he started public school. First I had to fight his father who believed that because he had a speech impediment that he didn't need education, that we should just keep him home and that later when he gets older that he would take him to Mexico to work on a ranch. I got tired of fighting him to help me get good resources for our son, so I separated from him.

Once my son got into special education, I kept close attention on the kind of education he was receiving. What I learned was that they didn't expect much of my son because he took longer to communicate verbally, so the teachers just had him counting plastic squares and I didn't see that he was learning much while at home I always read to him and found ways to help him communicate. However, when I would tell the teacher all of the things he was capable of doing, she said that she had special training with disabled children and she was just following the district policy. So I began to get active at the district level and working with parents who wanted the same things for their children. I kept visiting my son's classroom as often as I could while asking other teachers and the principal about what the best way was of getting disabled children to learn best. They kept pointing me to 'integrated instruction,' where children with learning disabilities would be integrated into regular classrooms. Those of us with English Learning (EL) children in learning disabled classes have been learning that many children can be reclassified into regular classrooms where they receive better instruction and have a better opportunity to get to college. We have fought at the district level to get bilingual special education students integrated and have succeeded in getting them integrated 70 percent. I'm so proud of him now that he's learning more English and is communicating better than ever before.

I began working with Mission Graduates because they have a good reputation in the community and I wanted to organize parents to help their children get to college. Then they began working with Believing the College Dream Program and I got even more excited about how it was necessary to organize parents to support their children get to college.

What I see that educators need to do is two things; one is to teach elementary-level students the same things that the parents are learning about how to get to college. The other thing is that educators also need to reach out to bilingual parents and motivate them to become more involved in the district-wide policy groups because that's where the important decisions are made on how our children are taught. And the more that parents get involved on how to help their children, the easier it is for teachers too because students do better in school when we're all working together.

An important lesson in Matilde's story is the importance of early focus on college for Latino children even in the face of adversity when students may be evaluated as underachievers or disabled. When parents are involved from the start of their children's schooling, they can intervene in the various obstacles that their children might face, which may become major obstacles to college if not addressed early.

Daniela, a single parent of five, became involved with Believing the College Dream through her work with Mission Graduates. She met the Mission Graduates coordinators through her work with Mission Health as a *promotora* (health aide), conducting workshops for middle and high school students.

(Translated from Spanish) I love working to organize parents. Since my children were very young, I encouraged them to go to school and get good grades, but my older sons did not go to college. I think if I had known about all the resources that were available to them, I would have pushed them more. Both of my sons are very successful now in their work, but they did not attend college. During their early years in school, I didn't know about all of the financial assistance until the oldest of my daughters came home and told me about a summer program that the Mission Graduates program was sponsoring. They were willing to pay most of the expenses if parents would help children to raise money for a few incidentals. My daughter was so excited that I was totally willing to support her because she knew in middle school that she wanted to be a pediatrician. I watched that she learned so much during that summer and she taught her younger sister everything she learned.

Wanting to learn everything I could about college, I got involved with Mission Graduates. They hired me to conduct workshops in the middle and high schools about the different programs about college that they sponsor. I have learned so much and all of that I share with my daughters. Now, both of my daughters are in college. One is at Whittier College and the other at UC Berkeley and they both have scholarships. Of course they have to work to pay for their personal incidentals. Now everything that my daughters know about going to college they tell my youngest son who is 16 years old. He also benefits from everything I'm learning about colleges from training other parents on Believing the College Dream.

> At first the teachers here didn't seem very interested in our Believing the College Dream training, but now one of the things that César Chavez has changed since we began training Latino parents here is that they now announce our Platicas over the intercom. This says to me that the school is beginning to recognize and value what we're doing. It would be good if they could teach everything we're learning in our Platicas to our children.

For many students like Daniela's daughters, middle and high school programs such as College Graduates inspire them to move forward in their dreams for a college education. However, not all Latino students have such programs available to them. This makes it imperative that parents have as much information as possible about the steps necessary about college because parents as well as educators the students' principal resources.

REFLECTION

College planning is a partnership between educators and parents. Neither one can do it alone because students need the total support and expertise of all the significant adults in their life. When schools engage parents beginning in the early grades, parents can assist children through their entire schooling. Most importantly, programs such as Believing the College Dream that have developed a systematic parent training for parents about college are an fundamentally important. Schools need to help create and support such programs in their respective communities.

BEST PRACTICES FOR SUCCESSFUL TEACHER AND PARENT PARTNERSHIPS

Facts From the Breakthrough Collaborative

- Educators need to help parents to monitor friendships and encourage connections with peers who plan to attend college. Students whose peers plan on attending college are 46 percent more likely to complete college.
- Students are four times more likely to enroll in college if a majority of their friends also plan to attend.

For Educators: Training Families to Prepare Students

- Educators need to train parents to help their children connect to school and locate community resources for academic support.
- Parents can also be employed to train other parents on topics related to college culture.
- Families need to be a part of their children's college search.

Components of Schools and Families Working Together

(*Believing the Dream, College Tools-ECM, 2009*; Believing the College Dream, 2012)

- Importance of a College Education
- Types of Colleges
- Finances
- Development of Academic Skills/Involving Parents in Homework
- Making Successful Transitions
- Utilizing Community Programs

Pre-Post Survey Sample
Questions—Center for Educational Partnerships

Parents/families understand financial opportunities available	*BEFORE TRAINING*		*AFTER TRAINING*	
	True	*False*	*True*	*False*
1. I know how to apply for financial aid.	29%	71%	71%	29%
2. For my child to apply for financial aid, they have to pay a fee.	0%	100%	14%	86%
3. If I or my family cannot afford to pay for college, my child will not be able to go.	19%	71%	14%	86%
4. Only students with the best grades qualify for financial aid.	14%	86%	0%	100%
5. There are many scholarships available that are not based on grades.	71%	29%	71%	29%

Source: Kaufman (2010).

Students Navigating the College Culture

9

Getting to college requires strong intention, discipline, and perseverance on the part of students. Although Latino students sit side by side with non-Latino peers that receive the same academic and college planning instruction in high school, some harbor questions or lack of understanding about participating in the mainstream culture. Latino students often have questions and concerns about college that educators may be unaware of because students do not know how to frame their queries. This chasm deters Latino students' admission or eventual college success because of underlying social and emotional differences in the way that they make meaning in their environment in contrast to their peers from mainstream families. To meet students' needs, educators need to become familiar with the way that decisions about college intersect with Latino students' personal and family life. As the college application process becomes more of a reality in high school, Latino students often confront situations where they have to represent their personal qualities in person or on paper.

ENDURING SOCIAL AND EMOTIONAL CHARACTER

From kindergarten through high school, educators work with Latino students in dreaming, thinking, and planning their college admission. Latino students need to think personally about themselves in planning their education. Students, particularly in middle and secondary levels, may have unexpressed feelings about their academic and personal abilities, talents, and the role of their family life and culture as they pursue their college path. Just as students need to develop academic skills, they also need to understand their social and emotional strengths. Educators and program planners need to help students discover their inner power and work with them to express those areas of their personal qualities that shape a strong sense of self and identity.

Self-assessment

A critical tool that college-bound students need is an honest self-assessment of their academic, social, and personal strengths and weaknesses. Knowing what attributes they can rely on in their personal skills puts students ahead in the college application game. However, some Latino students may live in families where calling attention to their strengths is discouraged because their cultural rules my value modesty over self-praise. This makes it necessary for educators to help students notice that recognizing their academic and personal attributes is part of their educational experience so that they can advocate for themselves when completing applications for special summer programs, scholarships, and college admission.

Educators play an important role in assisting students to take stock of their strengths from early grades to high school graduation. In the early grades, teachers can integrate students' self-esteem and valuation activities during language arts and literacy. Writing about their family, neighborhood, cultural activities, and favorite subjects helps Latino students reflect on their personal and cultural strengths.

In middle and high school years, counselors and other educators who coach students on their academics can work with Latino students to consider and evaluate their academic, social, and personal qualities. When students assess their strengths and needs, they become aware of their skills and can speak about them and present them fittingly to educators, parents, and in the college application process.

In the Redwood City, California Mother/Daughter Program, organized through the County Office of Education, mothers and daughters were socialized about the college culture. The director held Saturday workshops for mothers and daughters at the public library where mothers wrote about their daughters' skills. Mothers came together with daughters and read their story to their daughters. This was a personal way that girls learned to recognize their skills.

(Translated from Spanish) My dear Lupita, I know that you are very smart and I am very proud of you for all the things you are doing to get a good education. I know that not just me but your teacher, your father and even your brother appreciate that you're a hard worker.

You do all of your schoolwork at home without me reminding you and get very good grades at school. You're independent and you're able to care for your brother when he needs you like taking him to church on Sunday when your father and I work. You also care for others in the community when you help to organize other student to clean up our little park. You're very important to us, to the school, and the community. I will help you succeed in everything you want to do.

An example of an interaction of a mother reading to her daughter about her talents shows Mrs. Salinas sharing with Lupita, her sixth-grade daughter, what she felt were her gifts.

Lupita has a strong advocate in her mother who recognizes her academic skills, her willingness to work hard, her sense of responsibility in the family, and committed leadership in her community. These attributes are important self-knowledge that Lupita can learn about herself and become conversant with the college culture as she continues preparing for college in middle and high school.

Part of students' self-awareness includes their ability to advocate for themselves in public forums. When students attend informational meetings about colleges or special programs, even meetings with tutors and mentors, they are required to speak about themselves and their interests. Latino students may find these settings uncomfortable if they have not learned to talk about themselves in public. Their reluctance to do so may stem from feelings of modesty—that it is not proper for them to call attention to themselves. This makes it necessary for educators to prepare students in public speaking where they develop skills to represent themselves in public.

In a parent meeting, Rosa spoke about her daughter Becky's ability to speak up in a parent/student meeting they both attended. Rosa shared with the parent group,

I attended a meeting at a local college with Becky. The people at the meeting wanted the students to talk about their interests and why they would want to attend the summer career-planning program for middle school students. I was quite surprised when she raised her hand and spoke about her interest. She stood up very confidently and said, "I'm Becky and I am very interested in attending the summer program in your college because I want to be a pediatrician. However, I don't know everything that a pediatrician does and what I would actually do in that work. So, it's important for me to be in the program where I can learn what a pediatrician does every day and how they work with children and what they have to study in order to become a pediatrician. I really want to be a pediatrician to help children and the community." I was so proud of Becky because I had never heard her express herself so clearly about her plans for her career. And here she was standing in front of a room full of people. It showed me how important it is for our children to know how to express themselves and let people know how intelligent they are. I think it really helped the people at the college to know how serious she is about learning and that she would do very well in the summer program.

Rosa tells it proudly. It is important for Latino students to learn to represent their plans and interests in public settings. Becky shows that speaking up and sharing her story advances her opportunities. Thus, public speaking preparation needs to be a part of the college culture.

Family Ties

Educators need to work with both Latino students and the parents enabling both sides to know how to make an informed decision about a college. Assisting Latino students on how to involve parents in their decision about college means that educators need to know how Latino parents feel about allowing their children to attend a college away from home and how to support their children through the college application process. Of course, the earlier parents are informed about college in the early grades, the easier it is for them to help prepare their children for college throughout their schooling.

How families and communities respond to children leaving home sometimes has to do with where they live and what going away to college means to the family. Suárez-Orozco, Suárez-Orozco, and Todorova (2008) study Latino families from Spanish-speaking countries who leave their families to study in the United States. Although students may feel sad about leaving their family and community behind, they know that they'll return to help others in their family and communities to move ahead. For them, education is the means to improving their lives.

For other Latino families in the United States, the story differs in that students may want to go away to college, but parents object because they fear that children will forget about the family and stray from the culture, making it difficult to remain connected as a family. However, the experience can work out in a mutual understanding if educators discuss with parents a way to perceive college education as an advantage, not just to the student but to the family and community as well. In this case, the family sees itself as part of a larger community, where succeeding in school is part of an obligation and duty to the family. In this case, educators work with students and families to understand how education raises everyone's potential. Pride is a strong value in Latino families and communities, and students need educators' support to address their parents about the pride that they can share through a college education, thus helping the whole family advance their standing. Many students talk about returning to their family and helping them economically. Colleges do not have to be a time of separation between students and their families; it is an opportunity for parents to support children to work on everyone's behalf.

High school student Patricia's question to her counselor was, "*How do I tell my parents that it's important for me to go away to college?*" Patricia tells how her counselor helped her approach her family about going away to college.

My parents did not want to attend any school meetings about college. So when I was applying for schools where I could study science, particularly biology, it meant that, if I got accepted, I had to leave our small town to attend a larger university where biology had a large department. I had to explain to my parents why it was important for them to let me go away to college. They needed me to help them with my younger sisters. They thought I could stay near home to study in the community college since there was one near our home. My counselor was very helpful because she had been through the same situation with her parents. They were afraid that they would not see me again except for major holidays. When I explained to them that I could come home on vacations and work here or they could visit me sometimes too, they were a little more relieved. Of course, I had to remind them that I had to work on campus to earn money to make those trips home. I also told them that the most important reason that I wanted to go away to college was because they had a good science program. With this education, I could come back to my community and work in the medical clinics to help Latino children. They were a little more convinced that I was serious and not just going away to fool around. Of course, their questions continued almost daily after my talk with them, but I was able to answer them and it didn't seem like they were asking me questions to stop me from going. They just wanted all the information possible to feel more secure.

> I know they wanted me to help with my sisters so I told my counselor that they expected me to keep helping the family. She told me that I should assure them that I was not going to forget the family. I would always help my sisters to stay focused on their schooling and get good grades because I want them to get a good college education and plan for a good career.

Patricia's example is all too frequent with parents who fear that they're losing their children to another culture that they do not understand. However, as in Patricia's case, educators play a key role in helping students address the difficult issues with their families. Students need to know that when they go away to college that they can count on support from their family. Schools work with families to help them learn ways to understand the importance of students going away to college. Educators can help parents understand how stressful the college environment is for students. Latino students face a more arduous academic routine than they experienced in high school. They have to navigate a different social environment to connect with a supportive network. Some may also have to adjust to geography in a different state where the climate is quite different from the home state. When parents hear this information, they're able to recognize that students face a great deal of pressure and that they need to be a part of the supportive network for their children. Consequently, parents are less likely to expect their children, once in college, to assume family problems while they're away at school.

Ways that educators can assist students to communicate to parents and families about college plans involve bringing together the students with their families and people who can share their college experience. College students and community people have important insights to share with students and their families about college.

- Educators in middle and high schools can invite Latino college students to speak to students and parents about the reality of college life whether students live away or live at home while attending college.

- Latino parents whose children are already attending college away from home are also important resources for students and their families. Not only can they address the issue of children leaving home but they can also speak to the pressures of college even for children who choose to live at home.

- Counselors can also conduct workshops for parents on the way that students may feel guilt about leaving home if parents pressure them to stay strongly involved in the family's life. This pressure may ultimately take a toll on students' ability to do their academic work.

In these workshops, students from local colleges who may be living away from their home can address how they stay involved with their families and how parents can be most supportive. Educators can facilitate an important mentoring process by inviting college students and community members to speak with middle and high school students. Addressing Latino students' and their families' concerns about college involves open discussions about the matters. The most valuable information that students and their families can obtain is to realize that they can think differently about their fears that college would separate them from each other. Without a doubt, when Latino students leave for college or whether they live at home, changes occur in them and in the family. It's important for families to understand that those changes can enhance rather than threaten family relationships.

Students' Attitudes About Self

It is not often in schools that students hear from their teachers and other educators, "It's all right to make mistakes." True, some teachers allow for students to do trial-type activities, but when they receive a "C" or even a "D" on a test or even on their report card, Latino students may feel that they have failed. A negative self-appraisal can undermine students "forward looking" vision and confidence for their ability to attend college. How students view success and failure in their schoolwork matters as they move forward in their college planning. These issues of confidence and doubts affect students even more if they do not have an opportunity to express them and share them with others who may hold similar attitudes and doubts. Although many counselor and educators cannot work individually with students, there are strategies that students have identified as supportive for them in making these self-assessments. Student support groups on campus enable students to talk about their self-doubts and how to work through the areas of their academic or social life that become critical in planning for college and even more so once they are in college. Educators can sponsor and facilitate student groups.

To succeed in college, students need a healthy perspective about what success and failure mean for them. In their self-assessment, students need to understand that academic problems they may confront in college can have a successful resolution and are not a reflection of their ability. When students receive a disappointing grade, they need to learn how to move beyond an emotional response and find appropriate resources to bolster their skills, enabling them to perform better in the future. Chano's story illustrates a parent–child interaction about how students and parents can change beyond their cultural expectations and learn to find the resources to solve what could be a problem that affects his academic program. Chano recalls,

I was a sophomore in high school when I started to have problems in math. My mother had always paid attention to my sister's and my grades because she knew that they were important for us to get to college. But I didn't like algebra. I always tried, but I was never an "A" student in math. The quarter before the end of my sophomore year I got a "D" in pre-algebra. That really upset me. And my mother felt even worse. She immediately thought that she hadn't helped me enough and that I hadn't worked hard enough. But neither was true. Mom waited a couple of days before she talked to me about my poor grade in a math class. She was afraid that I may not get into the advanced math classes and she didn't know what to say. I felt really guilty about it, but I didn't know how to fix the problem either. Mom never talked to me about what to do when things go bad. And right now things were very bad and I didn't know how to fix this problem. Thinking back on this, I don't think she did either.

A few days later when mom did talk to me about the "D" in math, she told me that we had to go together to talk to my counselor. When we finally got an appointment, I was still having problems in my pre-algebra class. My counselor was really cool. She told mom that most of my grades were good and I was a good student. My mother told her that she thought that I had just gotten it into my head that I couldn't do math. I told the counselor that I didn't know what that meant, but I really didn't understand algebra. I know that my mom likes it when we get good grades, so I work hard to do it, but I've never really gotten a "D" and I didn't know what to do in this case where I disappointed my mother.

A meeting with Mrs. Vasquez, Chano's counselor, helped him and his mother take the next step in correcting the math grade problem. She asked Chano what he thought his problem was in math and he said that he didn't understand algebra even if he got good grades in other math before algebra. She also asked him why he was upset that he didn't get a good grade in algebra. Chano said that it upset his mother and that it would be difficult for him to get into college if he didn't get good grades in algebra. Chano's counselor told him,

The grade you can fix, Chano. You can get a good tutor. You can also change your grade by going to night school during the summer. You can take the class because we can't offer summer school classes here. But if you're really interested in going to college, we should talk about how you're going to make mistakes and get some things wrong many times in high school and in college. Maybe it'll be a low grade or in other ways, but it's bound to happen. When you get a low grade, you may feel disappointed if you worked very hard, but it doesn't mean that you're a poor student. It just means that you need to find out what it is that you need to do things differently. There are many ways to get people to help you. You haven't failed just because you got a poor grade. It just means that you need to find the people who can help you to get to your goal. So mistakes happen every day to all of us. None of us knows everything. Not me, not you and not your mother. But you need something you can reach out to people like myself or even your peers to help you. Even when we already have our careers like I have now, I still make mistakes and feel disappointed. But, that means that I just have to figure out what I need to do things differently and let others help me.

Mrs. Vasquez reminds Chano, and indirectly his mother, that mistakes are a part of the learning experience. The best that Latino students can do when they feel disappointed in an unexpected outcome, be it a grade or a personal relationship or even a family matter, is to reach out and communicate with a trusted adult and talk out the problem to find the possible solutions. In Chano's case, the knowledgeable expert was his counselor who could help him and the mother figure out how to improve his math skills. In others cases, knowledgeable others include parents, counselor, teachers, mentors, tutors, and informed peers.

Planning to Study

A component of college life that Latino students don't realize is important until it may be too late is *how to study* differently than they did in high school. In college, Latino students discover that they don't know how to organize the massive amount of work due without having someone remind them. Studying for courses in high school may come easy. In high school, teachers still remind students of due dates. They know students personally so they're apt to keep an eye on their progress. All that changes in college and often Latino students experience academic problems when they don't know how to organize themselves. They wrestle with understanding what discipline really means, how to locate resources if they need extra help, and how to organize a support group or find one where they can study with others. Learning to study in peer study groups has shown to be a learning strategy of successful students in college. For some Latino students, this becomes a problematic transition to college because they believe that they must succeed independently.

With a forward vision on what to expect in college, middle, and high school, educators can assist students to develop study strategies that build on their ability to work independently while creating support groups to support them. Learning how to pace their studying and to organize their time comes with the discipline of using a calendar to look at all the assignments and plotting the days and times devoted to study according to due dates. Using a calendar to plan which subjects to complete first, second, and third also eludes Latino students. This makes it necessary for them to learn how to plan short- and long-term completion of their assignments.

Latino students may not connect easily with educators in their school who can mentor them through the college planning process. This makes it necessary for them to reach out to community members in organizations or in other ways. Educators, however, can assist Latino students to find community mentors to value their talents and serve as links to the community where they may find mentors and build a team to assist students with talents that school staff may not be able to provide.

In Javier's example, he tells how getting involved in his diverse suburban community for extra credit during his high school freshman year turned out to be the best thing. Although he received good grades, Javier frequently found himself in trouble in school because he wouldn't follow rules and he refused to turn in some homework. All these infractions caused many conflicts at home with his mother who insisted that he get good grades and do everything right so he can get into a good college. Many times, Javier just wanted to draw. As part of a class assignment, he attended meetings of a family resource organization. He got involved with their group that met on Saturday mornings. While working in the community, he was able to learn a lot about working toward his success in college by creating a strong support group outside of school. He met peers who shared his passion in art, connections that he had not been able to make in school. Javier tells his story when he's a senior in high school, working on his college application.

When I entered this high school, I had to do volunteer work in the community, so my mother and sister always took me along with them to meetings and events in the community. For my community credit I decided to work with a community group that helps young people my age to learn how to organize community events such as cleaning parks, organizing workshops on underage drinking, doing a Christmas toy drive for families, and stuff like that. But what I got to do that was really cool was that I got to teach younger students how to do artwork. That's my thing. So, when I started doing it on weekends at the community center, some of the local artists paid attention and they brought other college students who were doing interesting art in their college. That was exciting because I could talk to them about art in a way that I didn't have someone like that in school. My mother thought this was a good thing too because she said that I wasn't as angry with her and my sisters as I had been.

Javier took his talent to the community and built a network of people who supported him, not just in mentoring him but also in focusing him to look forward to college and to take school seriously. He improved his high school experience while creating a team of people who were familiar with his work and would speak for him.

Latino students, who may not feel that they have a support network at school, need to reach out into the community even if the school does not require it. Educators, on the other hand, may find that community involvement credit for students serves a bigger purpose in building a college-bound network for them.

SUPPORT SYSTEMS FROM EARLY TO HIGH SCHOOL YEARS

No single method can possibly address the needs of the entire Latino student population, especially because the steps to socializing students for college span from elementary through secondary school. In the absence of a districtwide systematic college culture program, educators can implement specific approaches to address these social, cultural, and emotional issues pertaining to Latino students' personal identity and the various questions and concerns they harbor about college.

Elementary school–level educators utilize some very practical approaches to teaching young Latino students to discover their identity.

A popular literacy activity is the life story writing. At a small school in western Texas, third-grade teacher Mrs. Reyes engages her students to write about the things in their life that they're most proud of. This story is from Gloria, who writes,

---

The thing that I am most proud of is my grades. I get very good grades in my report card in all of my subjects. My mother is also very proud of me because I get very good grades. I like to make her happy and when I get good grades in my report card, she makes me my special dinner, enchiladas.

Another thing that makes me proud is how my parents help my brothers and me to do our homework. My brothers are older and sometimes they want to play sports and not do their work, but my parents make all of us do homework and chores around the house. They speak to us in Spanish and we have to speak Spanish too. I am proud that I can speak two languages because I can speak to my family in Spanish and to my friends in English. I also feel very proud that my mother says that she will help me to get to college because that way I can have a fun career and do work that helps my family and other Latinos. I don't know exactly what kind of career I want to have, but I do like people who report the news on television. Maybe I can do something like that. I know that I am proud of my grades and that I'm going to keep working hard and learning as much as possible. My teacher also helps me very much and I think she is proud of me too. She's very nice. [Mrs. Reyes edited the students' work.]

Observing how she feels about her academic performance and the people around her that she considers her support system moves Gloria forward with a vision for her future with personal attributes that she can count on. She appreciates her academic abilities and those around her that help her. In becoming aware of her academic strengths, she also recognizes that it requires hard work to accomplish it.

Although Gloria's parents are supportive, many cases exist where parents of ELL students do not know enough about the educational system to encourage their children. It is the ideal for students to be able to count on parental support throughout their educational career; however, it is possible for students who do not have total parental support and encouragement to pursue college. Fortunately, accessible and compassionate educators are available in programs that give ELL students a helping hand through the caring mentorship.

Middle school counselors play a critical role for Latino students. One-on-one conferences between counselors and students help students feel anchored into the culture of the school and provide educators with a personal portrait of student's performance and their college-bound status.

However, in middle school grades, identity and cultural issues arise that require involvement of other educators as well as community advocate groups such as Hispanic Outreach Center organized to support Latino youth. One such example of schools and community organizations collaborating comes from Tampa, Florida. Following Latino students' complaints of racial slurs hurled at them in Largo and Kennedy Middle Schools, educators convened youth support groups. Students were encouraged to speak in English although students could speak in Spanish when needed. Group curriculum includes teaching students social skills and conflict resolution so they can advocate for themselves. Students were able to raise family issues that many students shared in common, including having to care for younger siblings, which meant they missed school, thus affecting their academics negatively. In the groups, students improved their social skills and their communication with peers and with school staff (Cardenas, 2008). Latino students discussed the fact their English was limited and other non-Latino students teased them about this and made them feel isolated from English-speaking peers and school staff.

Students talked about issues in their family related to non-English-speaking parents and their low-socioeconomic condition that isolated them from the White community. In her student group, Monica shared that she had been absent recently because she had to translate for her father in court. She felt proud that she could speak English well enough to help her family. She recounts that a woman at the supermarket commented to her, "'I'm very proud of you. You are speaking English even though you are Hispanic.' My sisters, they were proud because we like to speak English" (Cardenas, 2008).

The Kennedy school principal believed that there was less tension on campus and credits the Latino student groups. School staff agrees, "The support groups have revealed the need for more bilingual teachers and staff at the schools."

A major consequence of the student group intervention at Largo Middle School was that they had the smallest number of out-of-school suspensions.

Middle school social and emotional issues that affect Latino students' academic performance need to be addressed aggressively, as the case in Largo and Kennedy Middle Schools illustrate through their collaboration with the Hispanic Outreach Center to organize the student youth groups.

High school can be a bewildering place for Latino students, especially since it is the final step before embarking on the college application process. Besides their academic performance, there are areas of mastery that students need to feel competent in, including leadership. High schools impose community involvement credit for students to acquire, which strengthens their college admission possibilities. Part of the leadership quality is caring about the well-being of others while working to create change in communities. Educators in some schools collaborate with community organizations that mentor students in their community leadership activities.

The Mother/Daughter (M/D) Program worked with fourth through sixth graders and their mothers in the elementary schools to develop college culture awareness through tutoring and mentoring. Although the program officially ended in the sixth grade for the girls, the director followed the girls into middle and high school grades. The M/D Program offered mentoring support to girls who volunteered in the community. Salina, a student who began working with the M/D Program as a fourth grader, wrote a story early in her M/D Program experience. She talked about wanting to be a marine biologist because she wanted to help clean the waterways and wanted to give back to her community that was surrounded by water. Salina got involved in her community, demonstrated her leadership skills in working with young Latino youth and helping them organize other youth to work against early alcohol use in their community. Although her community project was not directly related to her love of marine biology, she felt that working with her science group on campus fed her career interest. Meanwhile, she believed that it was important to develop youth consciousness and activism around an issue that plagued her low-income community. Salina's story describes her efforts in learning leadership skills in community boards and door-to-door canvassing for support of changing city ordinances.

I got involved with the John Gardner Center (JGC) when my science teacher told me how important it would be for me to get involved in something in the community that was not a high school or church group. She said that it was important for my college application, which I had to begin in two years. It seemed like a long time away, but my teacher said that credits add up the earlier I started.

At a community health fair, I met some of their leaders at a park. They were looking for signatures to organize a campaign against the overuse of public space for alcohol ads in our low-income neighborhood. They wanted to create a new ordinance limiting the number of ads in low-income communities by changing the required distance between alcohol ads. They especially wanted to increase the distance between ads and schools, churches, childcare centers, and our parks.

I got excited and told them that I wanted to volunteer to help because I knew that many young people in our school were having problems with underage drinking. They were happy to accept my help. My parents were very supportive that I wanted to volunteer with this group because it did good work to help communities. And the leaders really helped the student volunteers like myself. They drove me to all the evening and weekend meetings because I didn't drive. Sometimes the group leaders would give me a ride back home.

Soon after I began attending board meetings, they sent me to a workshop for student volunteers where they trained us to collect signatures at community events. JGC taught me how to do door-to-door outreach to inform people about the problems we had found in our communities that linked underage drinking with the crime that was increasing. I always had to go with adults, which was good. I was never scared. I loved doing the organizing work. I organized my friends at school so they could do outreach in their own streets and neighborhoods. It was slow work because it wasn't just a matter of collecting signatures. After that, we had to present them to the city council then wait for their decision. Then we had to present it to many other groups in the county. After that, we went before the Board of Supervisors.

Working with this group on the issue of underage drinking taught me not only to organize but I learned that change in communities takes a long time. And real change dealing with underage drinking didn't just mean telling students not to drink or hold workshops for students, which is what I thought we were going to do. It meant changing the policies and ordinances in our environment that caused a good deal of the problem. I still have a year before applying for college and I've already accumulated lots of hours of community credits because I love the project.

Although leadership is a lifelong process, Salina discovered the value of student volunteer work. Most importantly, she began learning that long-term change was not an instant process. It meant working to prevent the problem and not just addressing the symptoms. This too is a key feature of youth leadership work. She had three excellent resources to develop her leadership skills, supportive parents, supportive teachers, and a supportive community organization teaching her the process of working for change, which at times felt too far away to be attainable.

REFLECTION

From early grades to the college door, Latino students harbor questions about their identity, their language, respect for themselves and their family, as well as their status in the community. These social and emotional concerns need to be part of the school conversation alongside the academic achievement grades as students shape their vision toward college. How students make meaning of their feelings about their abilities, their family relationships, as well as their career and college choices does not have to wait until the college application process. From early childhood, students need the language and opportunity to speak about and discuss how their family and surroundings affect and support them. As students' worlds become increasingly complicated, there is a need for structured groups in schools as well as connections with community organizations to support the schools' efforts. When students feel safe in their family and school settings, they are able to focus on their academics and extend their leadership talents to the community.

Sites for Educators, ^{10} Students, and Families

President Obama said, "If we're serious about making sure that America's workers and America itself succeeds in the twenty-first century, the single most important step we can take is to make sure that every one of our young people . . . in the United States of America has the best education that the world has to offer" (Obama, 2010).

The college culture that many schools and communities have created offers great opportunity and promise for many students. The question is, why college? In the United States, college graduates earn 74 percent more than students who merely have a high school diploma. However, among Latinos, only 10 percent who enter a four-year college actually complete. It follows that educators need to prepare Latino students for college, beginning as early as kindergarten. This makes K–12 preparedness for college imperative for all students and specifically for Latinos. The global economy demands an educated workforce. And although Latinos have always been a large part of the U.S. workforce, many students from families who live in low-socioeconomic conditions have been undereducated such that they are unable to attend and succeed in college. This places professions requiring a college degree out of their reach. In a knowledge-based economy, the most desirable careers demand higher-order thinking skills that are emphasized in the Common Core Standards.

A college culture raises the bar in academic standards especially for Latino students, moving them out of a remedial curriculum to accelerated learning through enriched instruction as the Common Core Standards advance. Schools must create a college culture from kindergarten through high school, connecting students to broader community resources, university programs, and nonprofit organizations to maximize opportunities for educators and students. Some schools and national educational programs have developed ways to intervene and redirect the dismal educational trend with Latino students. Personal voices of students testify to their academic, social, and emotional development in effective college culture milieus. Many notable educational programs and schools described in this book share innovative curriculum, collaborative structures, and empowering parent engagement components. They shape the forward-thinking programs that support students on their path to college. In these settings, actors, including students, educators, and parents, act cohesively in creating a college culture.

Education opens opportunities for underrepresented groups to participate fully in their families and communities. Bridging educational inequities transforms community powerlessness to social justice. Without question, the overall economic health of the society depends on its educated workforce. When marginalized groups become empowered, they contribute to society. In turn, society benefits because the Latino immigrant group shows the fastest rise in birth rates than nonimmigrant mainstream groups. And a highly educated populace is an economic imperative.

With education as the engine of the country's economy, the United States must prioritize education for underperforming groups. It is in the interest of a democracy to have an educated citizenry that participates and serves in all areas of society. This positions education as a top critical social justice issue of the twenty-first century.

RESOURCES FOR CREATING
A COLLEGE CULTURE IN SCHOOLS

The resources included here provide information to educators, students, and parents involving the process of guiding Latino students to college with general information on maintaining a strong academic standing, completing the college application process, and obtaining financial assistance. Most of the websites are for middle and high school levels. Some sites for educators may be relevant for early elementary grades. Educators can use this chapter to provide students and parents with the resources for their respective groups.

The descriptions for each entry reflect some of the language of the respective resource. For example, if they indicated "Hispanic" I did not substitute the term with "Latino" although that is the term used consistently throughout the book.

- Four Steps to College for Middle and High School Students: This website helps students get information on how to reach out to mentors, the classes that count most toward college, and how to get the most from visits to colleges. Students are interviewed and share their personal experience. See Advancement Via Individual Determination (AVID) websites http://www.knowhow2go.org and http://www.knowhow2go.org/knowitall.

- Hidalgo Independent School District Toolkit: http://hidalgo.jff.org.
- *Hispanic Heritage Resources for Teachers*: Academic success of Latino students involves the inclusion of their rich heritage. The Teacher Vision Service provides printable plans, activities, and references that will enrich the daily classroom curriculum. Some of the activities easily integrate into literacy, literature, social studies, and more. http://www.teachervision.fen.com/hispanic -heritage-month/south-america/6629.html.
- *Incorporating Latino Parents Perspective into Teacher Preparation:* The Harvard Family Research Project website provides information for preservice educators on how to incorporate Latino parents' perspectives in the classroom curriculum. Parents believe that teachers need to learn about Latino neighborhood culture and language. Preservice teachers should learn and value children's individual personalities and differences. www.hfrp .org/family-involvement/publications-resources/incorporating -latino-parents-perspectives-into-teacher-preparation.
- *Latino Experience, Issues, and Resources:* This website offers a variety of papers on topics related to Latino student academic achievement. http://www.ithaca.edu/wise/latino/.
- *Latinos in College:* This website is an all-encompassing resource for assisting Latino students and their families in choosing schools, finding funding, and succeeding in college. It publicizes a corporate, public, and private program that benefits Latino students and their families. http://www.latinosincollege.com/ aboutus/.
- *Resources for Educators:* Fuente Press resources provides resources for educators teaching Latino students. http://www.dlenm.org/ index.php?option=com_content&view.
- *Science Education for Hispanic Students:* First-generation Latino students need a great deal of academic support in science to prepare them for advanced placements classes. This website informs educators on ways to increase effectiveness in their instruction. http://www.as.wvu.edu/~equity/hispanic.html.

RESOURCES FOR INFORMING STUDENTS AND FAMILIES

- *ASPIRA:* This organization promotes the empowerment of the Puerto Rican and Latino community by developing and nurturing the leadership, intellectual, and cultural potential of its youth so that they may contribute their skills and dedication to the fullest development of the Puerto Rican and Latino community everywhere. It is a very diverse and inclusive organization working with Puerto Ricans, Mexicans, Dominicans, Central Americans, South Americans, Cubans, as well as Native Americans, African Americans, non-Hispanic whites, and Haitians, among others. ASPIRA serves 65 percent females and 35 percent male students. http://www.aspira.org/en/manuals/who-do-we-serve-where-and-how.

- *Bridging Worlds:* This website features several articles by Catherine Cooper and her colleagues at the University of California, Santa Cruz, which focus on ethnic minority youth. Website at: www.bridgingworlds.org/selectedpublications.html.

- *Latino College Access Coalition:* This organization is a partnership of community groups where Latino students and parents can find expert advice on college planning, financial aid, and financial literacy. It provides a community-based environment of *Confianza*, which in Spanish means "Trust, comfort, and level of familiarity and knowledge that bespeaks confidence." This is an extension of the free program of the College Planning Center of RI, which has been providing college planning services for over 10 years. http://www.cpcri.org/EnEspañol/TheLatinoCollegeAccessCoalition/tabid/188/Default.asp.

- Planning for College in English and Spanish: (Español) http://mapping-your-future.org/espanol/, http://www.hsf.net/programs.aspx?id=750, and http://www.hsf.net/programs.aspx?id=734.

- *Report: Educating Latinos:* This is an NPR special report. NPR explores several topics about Latino education, including the bilingual education debate, educating Latinos, and the continuing achievement gap between generations of Latino immigrants. Available at: www.npr.org/programs/atc/features/2002/nov/educating_latinos/index.html.

- *Profile: Improving the educational profile of Latino immigrants.* Despite the persistence of an achievement gap between immigrants and native-born U.S. populations, this report finds that the educational profile of the adult population of Latino immigrants has improved in the past 30 years. This page also has a link to education data for California, Florida, Illinois, New York, and Texas. Available at: pewhispanic.org/reports/report.php?ReportID=14.

- *Report: College knowledge—What Latino parents need to know and why they don't know it.* This study highlights the levels of Latino parents' knowledge about preparing their children for college and includes recommendations to increase Latino college enrollment. http://www.pewhispanic.org/2002/07/30/latino-growth -in-metropolitan-america/.

INFORMATION ABOUT LATINOS IN COLLEGE

- *Report: Latinos in higher education: Many enroll, too few graduate.* This report considers the discrepancy between enrollment in higher education and degree completion for Latino students and suggests policy initiatives to address this problem. Available at: pewhispanic.org/reports/report.php?ReportID=11.
- *Report: Overlooked and underserved: Immigrant students in U.S. secondary schools.* This report describes the Program in Immigrant Education, its challenges, and schools' responses. Available at: www.urban.org/url.cfm?ID=310022.

FINANCIAL RESOURCES

Achieving the Dream

The Achieving the Dream scholarship competition is open to all students of Hispanic descent from Florida's First Coast, who will be at least a college freshman during the upcoming fall term. The applicant must be accepted to and planning to attend an accredited two or four-year college or university or currently enrolled as a full-time undergraduate or graduate student at an accredited institution, with a minimum GPA of 3.0. The applicant must not be more than a third-generation Hispanic with established home residency in the Florida First Coast region: Duval, St. Johns, Clay, Baker, or Nassau Counties for at least three years prior to the award date of the scholarship. http://www.scholarships.com/financial-aid/ college-scholarships/scholarships-by-state/florida-scholarships/achieving -the-dream/.

ACS Scholars Program

The basic criteria remain the same for all components of the American Chemical Society Scholars Program. To be considered a candidate, students should be African American, Hispanic/Latino, or American Indian; a U.S. citizen or permanent resident of the United States; a full-time student at an accredited college, university, or community college; high academic achievers in chemistry or science (grade point average 3.0, "B" or better). They need to demonstrate evidence of financial need and be a graduating high school senior. For details: http://portal.acs.org.

AMS Minority Scholarships

The AMS Minority Scholarships help support the college educations of minority students traditionally underrepresented in the sciences, especially Hispanic, Native American and African American students who intend to pursue careers in the atmospheric or related oceanic and hydrologic sciences. The two-year scholarships, funded by industry and through donations made by members to the AMS 21st Century Campaign, are for $3,000 for a nine-month period in the freshman year and an additional $3,000 for a nine-month period in the sophomore year. Minority students who will be entering their freshman year of college in the upcoming fall semester are eligible to apply. http://www.ametsoc.org.

Actuarial Diversity Scholarship

The Casualty Actuarial Society and the Society of Actuaries formed the Actuarial Diversity Scholarship in 1977 as a joint effort. Each applicant must have at least one birth parent who is a member of one of the following minority groups: Black/African American, Hispanic, or Native American Indian. A minimum GPA of 3.0 (on a 4.0 scale), with emphasis on math or actuarial courses, is required. High school seniors must have a minimum ACT math score of 28 or SAT math score of 600. The intent of pursuing a career in the actuarial profession is expected. For more information, visit The Actuarial Foundation website at http://www.actuarialfoundation.org.

AGI Minority Participation Program

Since 1972, the American Geological Institute has administered the Minority Participation Program. The broad goal for this program is to maintain and incrementally increase the number of underrepresented ethnic-minority students in the geosciences. Recipients of AGI Minority Geoscience Scholarships receive financial awards ranging from $500 to $3,000 and are given the opportunity to interact with a mentor from the geoscience community within our AGI MPP Advisory Committee. http://www.agiweb.org.

Alvarado/García Scholarship

High School Junior? Latino? College Bound? The Alvarado-Garcia Scholarship (AGS) in collaboration with the Association of Latino Men for

Action (ALMA) was established to recognize and foster outstanding gay, bisexual, and questioning Latino high school juniors who elect to attend an accredited two-year college or four-year university in Illinois. The AGS offers financial assistance and a mentoring program to support scholars who are capable of leadership in their chosen career. Recipients of the AGS are required to create an activity to bring awareness to GBQ issues in their community as well as keep in contact with mentors throughout their academic career. Scholars are eligible for $1,000 in financial assistance. http://almachicago.org/programs.php.

Berrien Fragos Thorn Arts Scholarships for Migrant Farmworkers

This scholarship is to foster and encourage the creative talents of students with a history of migration in agriculture. Eligible applicants must demonstrate an interest in pursuing further development of their talents in one of the following disciplines: visual arts, such as painting, sculpture, photography; performing arts—dance, theatre, music; media/film, video, animation, computer graphics; literary arts, including poetry, short stories; crafts—traditional folk arts, furniture, weaving, pottery. Application Criteria: Minimum 16 years of age. Visit: http://www.eduinreview.com/scholarships/berrien-fragos-thorn-arts-scholarships-for-migrant-farmworkers-218162/.

Catharine Lealtad Scholarships

Catharine Lealtad Scholarships are awarded to African American, Latino, and Native American students who have a strong high school record. The award is $3,000. Students who are National Achievement or National Hispanic Scholarship Finalists and who have a strong high school record will receive an annual award of $5,000. This scholarship is named for Dr. Catharine Lealtad, Macalester's first African American graduate. http://www.macalester.edu/admissions.

Edward S. Roth Manufacturing Engineering Scholarship

All applicants must be graduating high school seniors or current full-time graduate or undergraduate students seeking a bachelor's or master's degree in manufacturing engineering from an accredited school. All applicants must have and maintain a GPA of 3.0 or better on a 4.0 scale. Preferences will be given to students demonstrating financial need, minority students, and students participating in a Co-Op program. The scholarship can be used only as a credit toward books, fees, or tuition. Student must be a U.S. citizen. http://everyfuture.org.

Gates Millennium Scholars Program

The Gates Millennium Scholars (GMS), funded by a grant from the Bill and Melinda Gates Foundation, was established in 1999 to provide outstanding African American, American Indian/Alaska Natives, Asian Pacific Islander Americans, and Hispanic American students with an opportunity to complete an undergraduate college education in all discipline areas and a graduate education for those students pursuing studies in mathematics, science, engineering, education, or library science. For more information about the Gates Millennium Scholars Program, please visit: http://www.gmsp.org.

Getting Ready for College

Middle and junior high school students will find this a valuable resource on the steps to follow. It organizes the work of getting ready for and succeeding in college into a checklist. http://www2.ed.gov/pubs/GettingReadyCollegeEarly/index.html.

Haz La U/Make the U

Colgate proudly announces the return of its scholarship program "Haz la U" or "Make the U." This program, launched in partnership with the Hispanic Scholarship Fund (HSF), aims to award educational grants to eligible Hispanic students pursuing higher education. High school seniors are encouraged to apply for the opportunity to win a $15,000 educational grant or one of ten $2,500 additional grants. To apply, you must be of Hispanic American heritage and be a U.S. citizen or a legal permanent resident of the United States with a valid Social Security number at the time of application. http://oaklandtech.com/staff/scholarship/2009/09/30/haz-la-u-make-the-u-educational-grant/.

HEEF Friends of University of California Irvine Scholarships

The Friends of University of California Irvine Scholarships are to provide support for Hispanic high school seniors who are admitted and will attend the University of California, Irvine. Award Amount: $1,000. http://www.scholarships.com/.

HENAAC Student Leadership Awards

One undergraduate and one graduate student are selected annually to receive the HENAAC Student Leadership Award. Applicants must have demonstrated leadership through academic achievement and campus community activities. Applicants must be Engineering, Math, Computer

Science or Material Science majors, must have an overall GPA of 3.0, and be enrolled in an undergraduate or graduate program for the fall semester. Applicants must also be of Hispanic origin and/or must significantly participate in and promote organizations and activities in the Hispanic community. U.S. citizenship is not required. http://www.newvisions.org/henaac-student-leadership-%E2%80%A8award-scholarship.

Hispanic Scholarship Fund (HSF)

This fund works to address the barriers for deserving Latino students. The initiative is to strengthen the nation's future by ensuring that every Latino household in the United States will have at least one college graduate. http://www.hsf.net/.

Ohio Newspapers Foundation Minority Scholarship

Applicant must be a college-bound high school senior and enroll as a college freshman at an Ohio college or university for the coming school year. The applicant should be planning on majoring in journalism. A minimum GPA of 2.5 is required. Must demonstrate ability to write clearly in an autobiography of 750 to 1,000 words describing academic and career interests, awards, extracurricular activities, and any journalism-related activities. Applicant must be African American, Hispanic, Asian American, or American Indian. http://www.scholarships.com/financial-aid/college-scholarships/scholarships-by-type/minority-scholarships/asian-scholarships/ohio-newspapers-foundation-minority-scholarship/.

Hispanic Scholarship Fund (HSF) Money Manual

This publication focuses on managing your money for a college education. Its guide assists students in applying for college and for financial aid. http://www.hsf.net/publications.aspx (PDF format).

Maldef Scholarship Resource Guide

MALDEF has developed a Scholarship Resource Guide to support high school, college, and graduate students in their attainment of a higher education. This is a free, informative resource guide for students (including international students), parents, and educators. http://www.maldef.org/leadership/scholarships/index.html.

Magic Valley Electric Company

South Texas MVEC continues to support the youth of our area through a Scholarship Program for deserving high school seniors. Demonstrating the Co-op's commitment to education, scholarships are awarded to graduating seniors (including international students) in our service area each year. For eligibility requirements and application form, see website: http://www.magicvalley.coop/community/scholarship-program/.

Maldef Dream Act Student Activist Scholarship Program

MALDEF now offers a scholarship to support the nation's college and graduate student leaders who have been outstanding advocates for the DREAM Act and all immigrant rights. In 2012, MALDEF will offer scholarships of up to $5,000 each to deserving DREAM Act student activists. All current college and graduate students are eligible to apply. Students seeking to enroll in college or university for the first time (or to re-enroll following a leave of absence) are also eligible to apply. http://www.maldef .org/leadership/scholarships/index.html.

Middle and High School Students and Families Understanding College

This handbook helps families learn about the college requirements and work together to achieve graduation and admission to college. Materials are provided in both English and Spanish. http://www2.ed.gov/ pubs/GettingReadyCollegeEarly/step1.html.

Road to College

This website helps families understand what needs to be done in high school to prepare for college admissions. College Roadmap: http://www .collegeroadmap.com/.

Ronald McDonald House Charities HACER Scholarship Program

These scholarships are part of the charities' ongoing commitment to education. Eligibility: Currently enrolled high school seniors who have at least one parent of Hispanic heritage and who are eligible to attend a two or four-year college, university, or vocational/technical school with a complete course of study. Applicants must be legal U.S. residents, be less than 21 years of age and reside within the geographic boundaries of a participating school. Scholarship recipients must enroll in and attend a two or four-year accredited college or university or vocational/technical school in the academic year following their selection. http://931amor .com/blogs/djs/hacer-the-ronald-mcdonald-house-charities-hispanic -scholarship-program.

RTNDA Carole Simpson Broadcast Journalism Scholarship

Carole Simpson, ABC news senior correspondent, created this annual $2,000 award to encourage and help minority students overcome hurdles along their career path. Besides honoring those with talent, Carole is strict about her applicants meeting requirements in tenacity, determination, and ambition to excel. http://www.scholarships.com/financial-aid/college-scholarships/scholarships-by-type/minority-scholarships.

RTNDA Ed Bradley Broadcast Journalism Scholarship

A $10,000 award was established by *60 Minutes* correspondent Ed Bradley. Preference is given to an undergraduate student of color. Career goal must be broadcast journalism. Applications must be postmarked on or before May deadline. http://www.rtdna.org/pages/media_items/ed-bradley-scholarship1898.php.

TELACU Scholarship Program

Each year, the TELACU Education Foundation awards hundreds of scholarships to students in California, Texas, Illinois, and New York. To apply for a scholarship, download the application from our website and return it, with required attachments, to the office indicated on the application. Minimum eligibility requirements: Must be a low-income, first-generation college student. Students must also be a full-time student for the entire coming academic year. http://telacu.com/site/en/home/education/applications.html.

The Jackie Robinson Foundation

The Jackie Robinson Foundation scholarship application will be available online. Only online applications are accepted. Follow the online instructions. Applicants must be minority students at a high school level and preparing to attend a four-year accredited college or university, SAT score of 900 or above, and/or ACT score of 19 or above. http://www.jackierobinson.org/apply/programs.php.

Workshops for Applying for Scholarships

Hispanic Scholarship Fund (HSF) tours the country bringing educational outreach programming to communities across America. http://www.hsf.net/workshops.aspx.

References

Allen, W. R., Bonous-Hammarth, M., & Suh, S. A. (2003). Who goes to college? High school context, academic preparation, the college choice process, and college attendance. In E. P. St. John (Ed.), *Readings on equal education* (Vol. 20, pp. 71–113). New York, NY: AMS Press.

Auerbach, S. (2004). Engaging Latino parents in supporting college pathways: Lessons from a college access program. *Journal of Hispanic Higher Education, 3*(2), 125–14.

AVID. (2011). Pleasant Valley Middle School AVID: A case study in equity and rigor for all. Retrieved from http://www.avid.org/dl/resources/bp_case_pleasantvalleyms.pdf

AVID. (2012). Decades of college dreams. Retrieved from http://www.avid.org/

Belohlav, K., & Brown, C. (2012, May). *Readymade analysis of Berkeley Scholars to Cal program.* Retrieved from Center for Work Technology and Society, IRLE, University of California, Berkeley website: http://escholarship.org/uc/item/35v53265

Blanc, R., DeBuhr, L, & Martin, D. (1983). Breaking the attrition cycle: The effects of supplemental instruction on undergraduate performance and attrition. *Journal of Higher Education, 54*(1), 80–90. Retrieved from http://www.jstor.org/stable1981646

Boden, K. (2011). Perceived academic preparedness of first-generation Latino college students. *Journal of Hispanic Higher Education, 10,* 96–106.

Breakthrough Collaborative. (2012). Retrieved from http://www.breakthrough-collaborative.org/breakthroughs/reflections

Breakthrough Santa Fe. (2012). Retrieved from http://www.breakthroughsantafe.org/index.php/teachers/C6/

Burris, C., & Garrity, D. T. (2012). *Opening the common core: How to bring all students to college and career readiness.* Thousand Oaks, CA: Corwin.

Cabrera, A. F., & La Nasa, S. M. (2000). *Understanding the college choice of disadvantaged students: New directions for institutional research.* San Francisco, CA: Jossey-Bass.

Cardenas, J. (2008, May 6). Ending feelings of isolation for hispanic students. *Tampa Bay Times.* Retrieved from http://www.tampabay.com/news/humaninterest/ending-feelings-of-isolation-for-hispanic-students/489956

Cardona, M. T. (2009, March 5). Majority/near-minority of first graders in top ten U.S. cities are Latinos. La Plaza. [Web blog post]. Retrieved from http://blog.latinovations.com

Cavazos., A. G, & Cavazos, J. (2010, Spring). Understanding the experiences of Latino students: A qualitative study for change. *American Secondary Education, 38,* 95–109.

Ceja, M. (2006). Understanding the role of parents and siblings as information sources in the college choice process of Chicana students. *Journal of College Student Development, 47*(1), 87–104.

Chapa J., & De La Rosa, B. (2004). Latino population growth, socioeconomic, demographic characteristics, and implications for educational attainment. *Education and Urban Society, 36,* 130–149.

College Board. (2011). Retrieved from http://www.collegeboard.com/student/plan/high-school/50432.html

Collier, V. P., & Thomas, W. P. (2009). *Educating English learners for a transformed world.* Albuquerque, NM: Fuente Press.

Cooper, R., & Markoe-Hayes, S. (2005). *Improving the educational possibilities of urban high school students as they transition from 8th to 9th grade* (PB-013-0905). Retrieved from UC/ACCORD Public Policy Series, UCLA website: http://ucaccord.gseis.ucla.edu/publications/pdf/pb-013-0905.pdf

Darder, A. (2012). *Culture and power in the classroom: Educational foundations for the schooling of bilingual students.* Herndon, VA: Paradigm Publishers.

Delgado Gaitan, C. (2001). *The power of community: Mobilizing for family and community.* Boulder, CO: Rowman & Littlefield.

Delgado Gaitan, C. (2004). *Involving Latino families in schools: Raising students' achievement through home-school partnerships.* Thousand Oaks, CA: Corwin.

Dougherty, C., Mellor, L., & Jian, S. (2006, February). *National Center for Educational Accountability: Ensuring that "Advanced Courses" live up to their labels* (NCEA Policy Brief No. 1). Retrieved from http://hub.mspnet.org/index.cfm/12852

Downtown College Prep. (2008). Retrieved from http://www.dcp.org/content/pauline-fernandez-class-2008

Downtown College Prep. (2011). Retrieved from http://bestpractices.dcp.org/dcp_staff_bios.php

East Bay Consortium. (2011). *I'm Going to College Program* [Utube movie]. Retrieved from http://www.eastbayconsortium.org/

ECMD Foundation. (2012). Believing the college dream curriculum. Retrieved from www.ecmcfoundation.org

Edelstein, W. (2010, March 9). Berkeley Scholars to Cal works to close the achievement gap. *UC Berkeley News Center.* Retrieved from http://newscenter.berkeley.edu/2010/03/09/scholars/

Engle, J., Bermeo, A., & O'Brien, C. (2006). *Straight from the source: What works for first-generation college students.* Report of the Pell Institute For the Study of Opportunity in Higher Education. Retrieved from http://www.pellinstitute.org/

Family School and Community Engagement—FINE. (2011, June 23). *Successful transitions to high school: Promoting success and facilitating college readiness* [Video file]. Retrieved from http://www.youtube.com/watch?v=llAYzMU2rdQ

Fine, M. (1991). *Framing dropouts: Notes on the politics of an urban high school.* New York, State University of New York Press.

First Generation College Bound, Inc. (2012). Retrieved from http://www.fgcb.org

Fisher, D., & Frey, N. (2011). Academic language in the secondary classroom. *Principal Leadership, 11*(5), 58–60.

Freedman, T., & Mandelbaum, M. (2011). *That used to be us: How America fell behind in the world and how we can come back.* New York, NY: Farrar, Straus, and Giroux.

Fry, R. (2000). *Latinos in higher education: Many enroll, too few graduate.* Retrieved from the Pew Hispanic Center website: http://www.chavezcenter.org/pdf/education/latinos-in-higher-education.pdf

Fry, R. (2006). *Are immigrant youths fairing better in U.S. schools.* Paper presented at the 2006 Population Association of America Meetings, Los Angeles, CA.

Fry, R. (2008). *Latino settlement in the new century.* Report of the Pew Hispanic Center. Retrieved from http://pewresearch.org/pubs/1002/latino-population-growth

Fry, R., & Gonzalez, F. (2008). *One in five and growing fast: A profile of Hispanic public school students.* Report of the Pew Hispanic Center. Retrieved from www.pewhispanic.org

Fuller, M. L., & Olsen, G. (1998). *Home-school relations: Working successfully with parents and families.* Boston, MA: Allyn Bacon.

Gándara, P. (2010). The Latino education crisis. *Educational Leadership, 6*(5), 24–30.

Gándara, P. (2011). Role of parents and family. Retrieved from http://www.puente.net/programs/family_role.html

Gándara, P., & Biel, D. (2001). *Paving the way to postsecondary education: K–12 intervention programs for underrepresented youth* (Report No. NCES 2001205). Prepared for the National Postsecondary Education Cooperative Access Working Group. Washington, DC: U.S. Department of Education, National Center for Education Statistics.

Garcia-Reid, P., Reid, R., & Peterson, N. A. (2005, May). School engagement among Latino youth in an urban middle school context: Valuing the role of social support. *Education and Urban Society, 37*(3), 257–275.

GEAR UP. (2012). Oklahoma GEAR UP. Retrieved from www.okhighered.org/gearup

GEAR UP. (2012). Massachusetts GEAR UP Video. Retrieved from www.gearup.mass.edu/vidos.aspx

Gonzalez, K. P., Stoner, C., & Jovel, J. (2003). Examining the role of social capital in access to college for Latinas: Toward a college opportunity framework. *Journal of Higher Education, 2*, 146–170.

González, V. (2009). Language, culture, and cognition: From research to improving educational practice for Latino students. In, Murillo, E. G., Villenas, S., Galvan, R. T., Muñoz, J. S., Martínez, C., & Machado-Casas, M. (Eds.), *Handbook on Latinos in education.* New York, NY: Routledge.

Greene, J. P. (1998). *A meta-analysis of the effectiveness of bilingual education.* Policy paper sponsored by the Tomas Rivera Policy Institute, the Public Policy Clinic of the Department of Government, University of Texas at Austin, the Program of Education Policy and Government at Harvard University. Retrieved from http://www.hks.harvard.edu/pepg/PDF/Papers/biling.pdf

Hamilton, R. (2010, December 24). Early college concept takes hold in Hidalgo. *The Texas Tribune,* 13.

Haycock, K. (2001). Helping students achieve: Closing the achievement gap [online document]. Retrieved from http://www.cdl.org/resource-library/articles/achieve_gap.php

Hidalgo School District. (2011). Hidalgo early college toolkit. Retrieved from http://hidalgo.jff.org/

Hyde Square Task Force. (2012). *History of program.* Retrieved from http://www.hydesquare.org/about_us/history.html

Hyde Square Task Force. (2012). *Program.* Retrieved from http://www.hydesquare.org/programs/education.html

Immerwahr, J. (2003). *With diploma in hand: Hispanic high school seniors talk about their future* (National Center Report #03–2). Retrieved from http://www.highereducation.org/reports/hispanic/hispanic.shtml

Immerwahr, J., & Foleno, T. (2000, May). Great expectations: How the public and parents—White, African American and Hispanic—view higher education. Report by Public Agenda Research Studies. Retrieved from http://www.highereducation.org/reports/expectations/expectations.shtml

Jager-Hyman, J. (2008). *Fat envelope frenzy: One year, five promising students, and the pursuit of the Ivy League prize.* New York, NY: Harper.

Jarsky, K. M., McDonough, P. M., & Nuñez, A-M. (2009). Establishing a college culture in secondary schools through P–20 collaboration: A case study. *Journal of Hispanic Higher Education, 8*(4), 357–373.

Kaufman, G. (2010). *Survey results from 2009–2010: Destination College Advising Corps Program.* Supported by the Doris and Donald Fisher Fund, Center for Educational Partnership. Berkeley: University of California.

Koebler, J. (2011, June 13). National high school graduation rates improve. *The Chronicle of Higher Education.* Retrieved from https://chronicle.com/article/latinos-need-more-support-to/129247/

Levin, H. M. (1998). *Accelerated schools for at-risk students* (Report No. 142). New Brunswick, NJ: Rutgers University.

Lopez, M. H. (2009, October 7). Latinos and education: Explaining the attainment gap. *Pew Research Center.* Retrieved from http://www.pewhispanic.org/2009/10/07/latinos-and-education-explaining-the-attainment-gap/

Losey, K. (1995). Mexican American students and classroom interaction: An overview and critique. *Review of Educational Research, 65*(3), 283–318.

Lozano, A. (2008, Winter). A personal charge to defy the odds and close the achievement gap. *ACCESS, 14,* 2–3.

Martinez, M. D. (2003). Missing in action: Reconstructing hope and possibility among Latino students placed at risk. *Journal of Latinos and Education, 2*(1), 17.

Martínez, V. R. (2008, Winter). How one school is helping Latino ELL students through AVID. *ACCESS, 14,* 8–9.

McDonald, M. F., & Dorr, A. (2006). *Creating a college going culture: A resource guide.* Los Angeles, CA: Academic Preparation and Educational Partnerships, UCLA.

McDonough, P. M. (2005). Counseling matters: Knowledge, assistance, and organizational commitment in college preparation. In W. G. Tierney, Z. B. Corwin, & J. E. Colyar (Eds.), *Preparing for college: Nine elements of effective outreach,* 69–88. Albany, NY: SUNY Press.

McDonough, P. M. (2008). Building a college culture: Goals, principles, and a case study. Retrieved from http://www.inpathways.net/ipcnlibrary/ViewBiblio.aspx?aid=8439

McDonough, P. M. (2009). Building a college culture: Needs, goals, principles, and a case study. Retrieved from http://collegetools.berkeley.edu/resources.php?cat_id=9#top

McKown, C., & Weinstein, R. S. (2008). Teacher expectations, classroom context and the achievement gap. *Journal of School Psychology, 46*(2), 235–261.

National Center for Educational Statistics. (2012). Retrieved from http://nces.ed.gov/collegenavigator

National Commission on Excellence in Education. (1983, April). *A nation at risk—an open letter to the American people. The imperative for educational reform.* Retrieved from http://www.edweek.org/ew/articles/1983/04/27/03170033.h02.html

National Governors Association Center for Best Practices, Council of Chief State School Officers. (2010). *Common Core State Standards.* Washington, DC: Author.

Nodine, T. (2010, October). *College success for all: How the Hidalgo Independent School District is adopting early college as a district-wide strategy* [Online report]. Retrieved from http://hidalgo.jff.org

Noguera, P. (2008, June 10). A broader, bolder approach to education. *The Huffington Post.* Retrieved from http://www.huffingtonpost.com/pedro-noguera/a-broader-bolder-approach_b_106244.html

Noguera, P., & Williams, J. (2010, Winter). Poor schools or poor kids? Retrieved from Education Next website: http://educationnext.org/files/ednext_20101_44.pdf

Oakes, J. (1995). Two cities' tracking and within-school segregation. *Teachers College Record, 96*(4), 681–690.

Obama, B. (2010, August 9). Education is economic issue: President Obama speaks at the University of Texas in Austin, Texas. *Politico.* Retrieved from http://www.politico.com/news/stories/0810/40832.html

Pathways to College Network. (2004). *A shared agenda: A leadership challenge to improve college access and success.* Retrieved from website: http://www.pathwaystocollege.net.

Perna, L. W. (2002). Pre-college outreach programs: Characteristics of programs serving historically underrepresented groups of students. *Journal of College Student Development, 43*, 64–83.

Pew Hispanic Organization. (2008). U.S. Populations Projection (2005–2050). Retrieved from www.pewhispanic.org/reports

Pew Hispanic Organization. (2011). Hispanic student enrollments reach new highs in 2011. Retrieved from http://www.pewhispanic.org/files/2012/08/Hispanic-Student-Enrollments-Reach-New-Highs-in-2011_FINAL.pdf

Powell, M. A. (1997). *Peer tutoring and mentoring services for disadvantaged secondary school students* (CRB Note vol. 4, no. 2). Report from the California Research Bureau, California State Library website: http://www.library.ca.gov/CRB/97/notes/v4n2.pdf

Price, E. J. (2010, August 7). U.S. needs a college culture. *Dallas Morning News,* 1–2.

Puente Project. (2011). Retrieved from http://www.puente.net/about/governance.html

Quijada, P. D., & Alvarez, L. (2006). Understanding the experiences of K–8 Latina/o students. In J. Castellanos, A. M. Gloria, & M. Kamimura (Eds.), *The Latina/o path to the Ph.D.* (pp. 3–17). Sterling, VA: Stylus Publishing.

Reed, C. (2010, March). Rising to the challenge of improving higher education for Latinos. *Tomas Rivera Lecture Series.* Conducted at the meeting of American Association of Hispanics in Higher Education, ETS, Princeton, NJ.

Reis, S. M., Gentry, M., & Maxfield, L. R. (1998). The application of enrichment clusters to teachers' classroom practices. *Journal for Education of the Gifted, 21,* 310–324.

Reisner, E. R., Petry, C. A., & Armitage, M. (1989). *A review of programs involving college students as tutors or mentors in grades K–12.* Paper prepared by Policy Studies Associates, Inc. for the U.S. Department of Education, Washington, DC.

Roberts, M. B. (2009, October). JUNTOS: Together Realizing Our Potential. *AVID National Conference.* San Antonio, TX.

Schott Foundation for Public Education. (2009). *An opportunity for every child: Recommendations for federal action to provide all students a fair and substantive opportunity to learn.* Cambridge, MA: Author.

Suárez-Orozco, C., & Suárez-Orozco, M. (1995). *Transformations: Immigration, family life, and achievement motivation among Latino adolescents.* Stanford, CA: Stanford University Press.

Suárez-Orozco, C., Suárez-Orozco, M., & Todorova, I. (2008). *Learning a new land.* Cambride, MA: Harvard University Press.

Swail, W. S., Cabrera, A. F., & Lee, C. (2004). *Latino youth and the pathway to college.* Retrieved from Pew Hispanic Center website: http://www.pewhispanic .org/files/reports/31.pdf

Tauber, R. (1997). *Self-fulfilling prophecy: A practical guide to its use in education.* Westport, CT: Praeger.

Tenenbaum, H. R., & Ruck, M. D. (2007). Are teachers' expectations different for racial minority than for European American students? A meta-analysis. *Journal of Educational Psychology, 99*(2), 253–273.

Todorova, I., & Suarez-Orozco, C. (2002). *Changing countries, changing stories: Immigrant children's narratives projected with the Thematic Apperception Test.* Paper presented at the Murray Research Center Lecture Series, Radcliffe Institute for Advanced Study, Cambridge, MA.

Turner, R. (2008). *Great expectations.* Portland, ME: Stenhouse.

United States Census Bureau. (2010). *Profile America Facts for Features: Hispanic Heritage Month 2010: September 15–October 15.* Retrieved from http://www .census.gov/newsroom/releases/archives/facts_for_features_special_ editions/cb10-ff17.html

United States Bureau of the Census (2000–2008). *Population trends.* Washington, DC: Government Printing Office.

United States Department of Education. (1999). *What works for Latino youth. White House initiative on educational excellence for Hispanic Americans, second edition.* Washington, DC: white House Initiative on Educational Excellence for Hispanic Americans, U.S. Department of Education, National Center for Education Statistics, Institute of Education Science.

United States Department of Education Office of Under Secretary Policy and Program Studies Service. *National evaluation of GEAR UP: A summary of the first two years* (Doc. No 2003-13). Retrieved from http://www2.ed.gov/rsch-stat/eval/highered/gearup.pdf

Vasquez, O. A. (2007). Technology out of school: What schools can learn from community-based technology. *Yearbook of the National Society for the Study of Education, 106*(2), 182–206.

Verdugo, R., & Glenn, B. C. (2006, February). *Race and alternative schools.* Paper presented at the annual meeting of the Alternatives to Expulsion, Suspension, and Dropping Out of School Conference, Orlando, FL.

Walsh, J. A., & Sattes, B. D. (2005). *Quality questioning: Research-based practice to engage every learner.* Thousand Oaks, CA: AEL and Corwin.

Williams, J. (2008). Educational equity project. Retrieved from www.educationequalityproject.org

Yeung, B. (2009, August 3). *The Puente project prepares Hispanic teens for college success. What works in education.* Edutopia: The George Lucas Educational Foundation. Retrieved from http://www.edutopia.org/

Zwiers, J. (2007). *Building academic language: Essential practices for content classrooms, grades 5–12.* San Francisco: Jossey-Bass.

Index

CORWIN
A SAGE Company

The Corwin logo—a raven striding across an open book—represents the union of courage and learning. Corwin is committed to improving education for all learners by publishing books and other professional development resources for those serving the field of PreK–12 education. By providing practical, hands-on materials, Corwin continues to carry out the promise of its motto: **"Helping Educators Do Their Work Better."**